POO WITH A VIEW

High Alpine Shitters of the Canadian Rockies

GAVIN T BOUTET

Poo With a View
Copyright © 2020 by Gavin T Boutet

All rights reserved. No part of this publication may be reproduced, distributed, or transmitted in any form or by any means, including photocopying, recording, or other electronic or mechanical methods, without the prior written permission of the author, except in the case of brief quotations embodied in critical reviews and certain other non-commercial uses permitted by copyright law.

tellwell

Tellwell Talent
www.tellwell.ca

ISBN
978-0-2288-2486-2 (Hardcover)
978-0-2288-2485-5 (Paperback)

Spending a night or two in the wilderness without the comforts of home can create the simplest of pleasures. I can attest to any facility being better than none, especially when it comes to shitting in the woods.

In the rugged wilderness of the Canadian Rockies, I believe the outhouse is often the unsung hero. This collection celebrates my favourite backcountry thrones in the region and presents them without you having to plug your nose. Wherever you are, I hope that you are comfortable and can enjoy the views.

Poo With a View
Gavin T Boutet

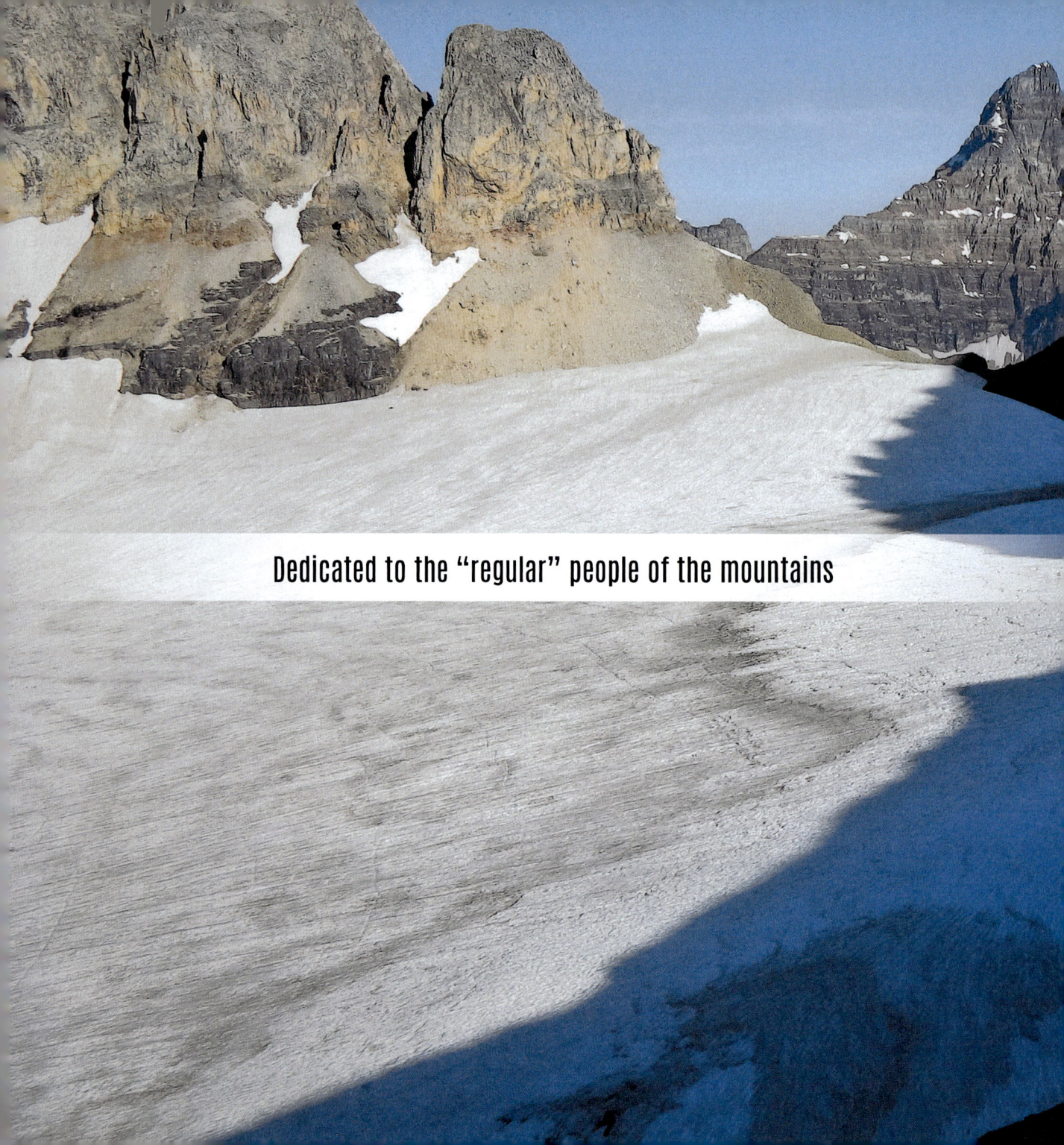
Dedicated to the "regular" people of the mountains

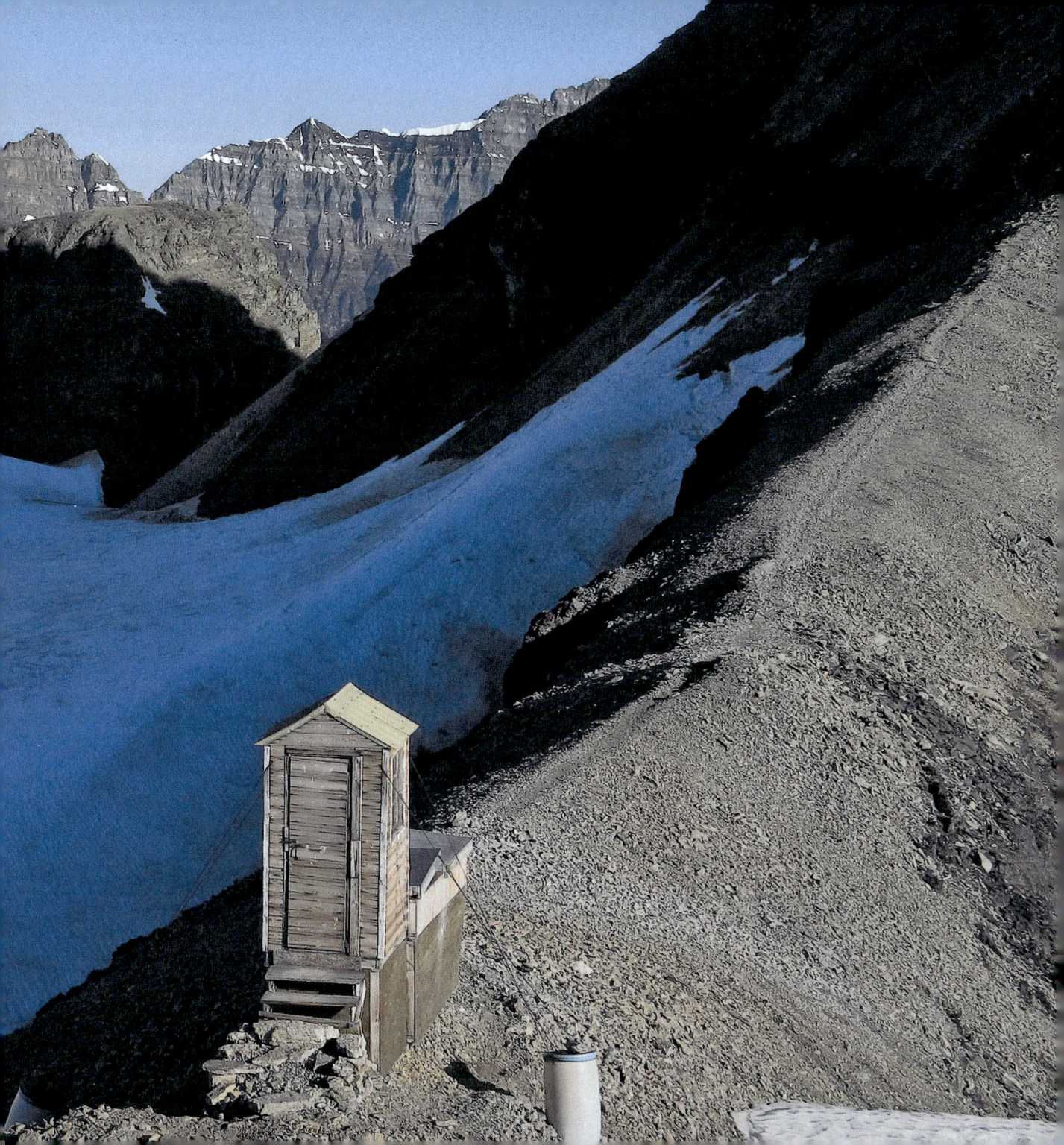

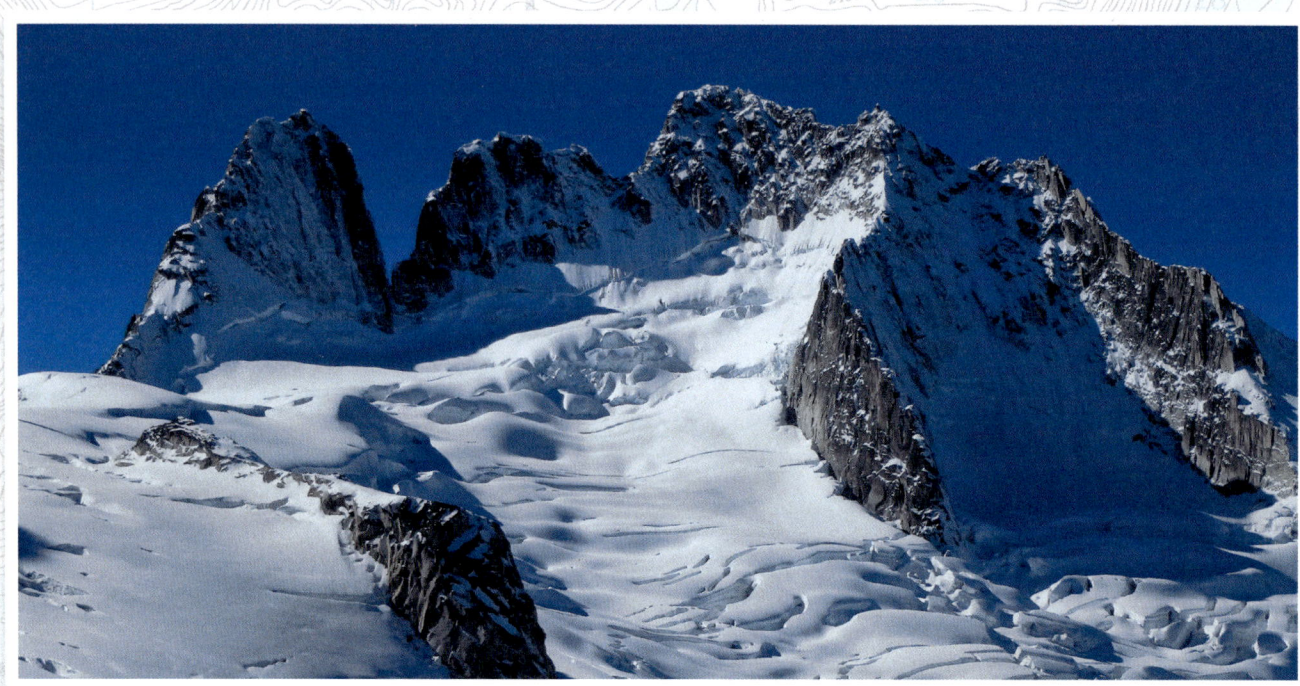

Poo With a View
Gavin T Boutet

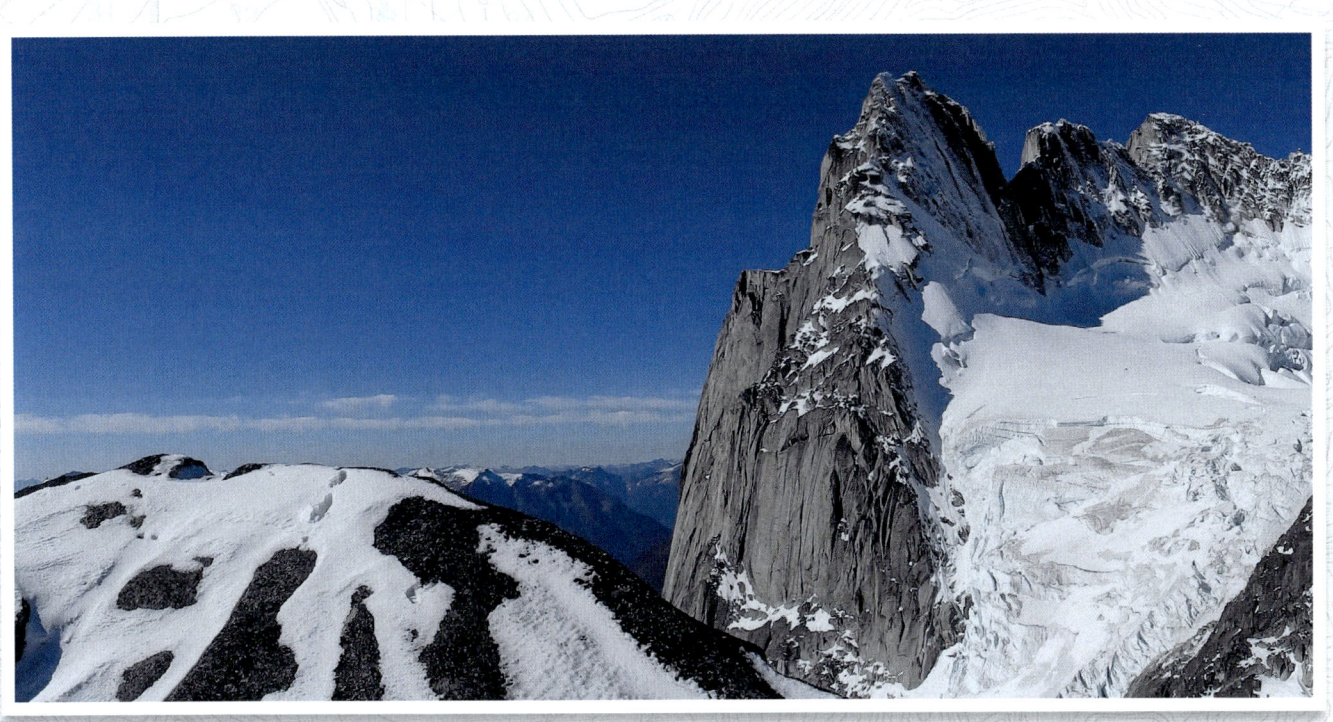

Poo With a View
Gavin T Boutet

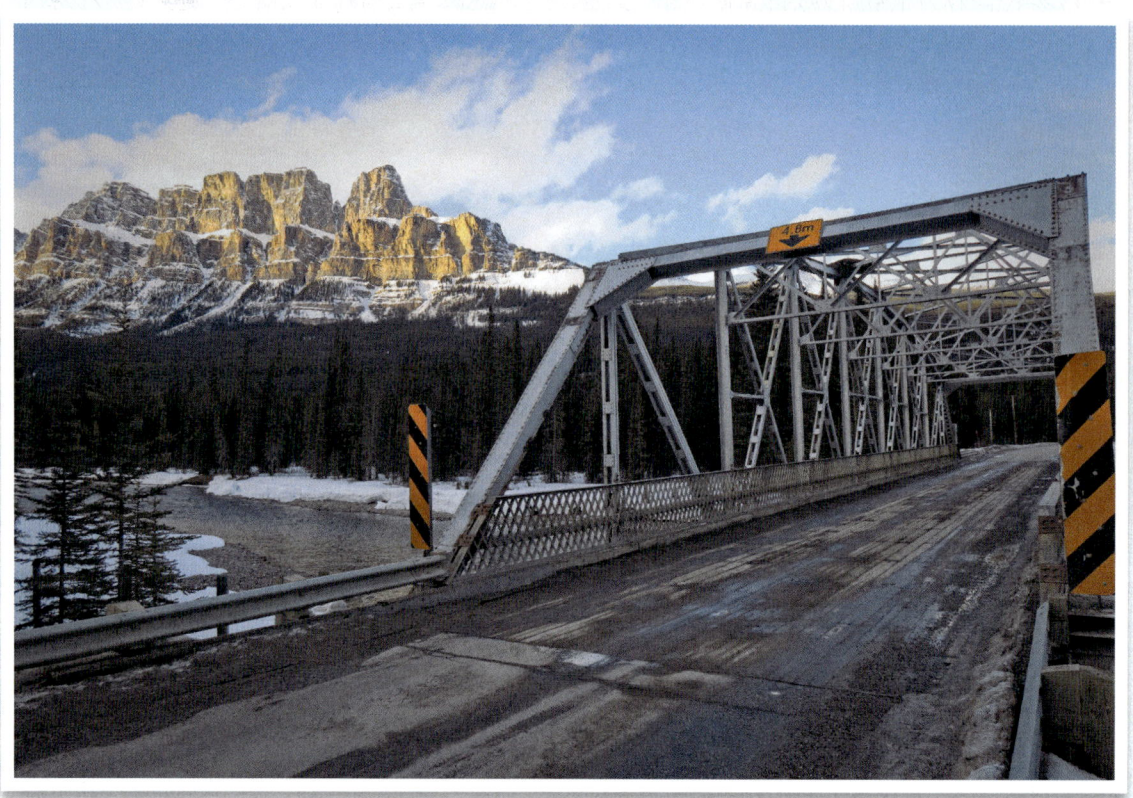

CASTLE MOUNTAIN

2,390 m (7,841 ft)
Banff National Park, Alberta

Perched on Goat Plateau halfway up Castle Mountain lies this "open-air" potty. It's an A+ experience in good weather that offers stunning views of both Banff and Kootenay National Parks.

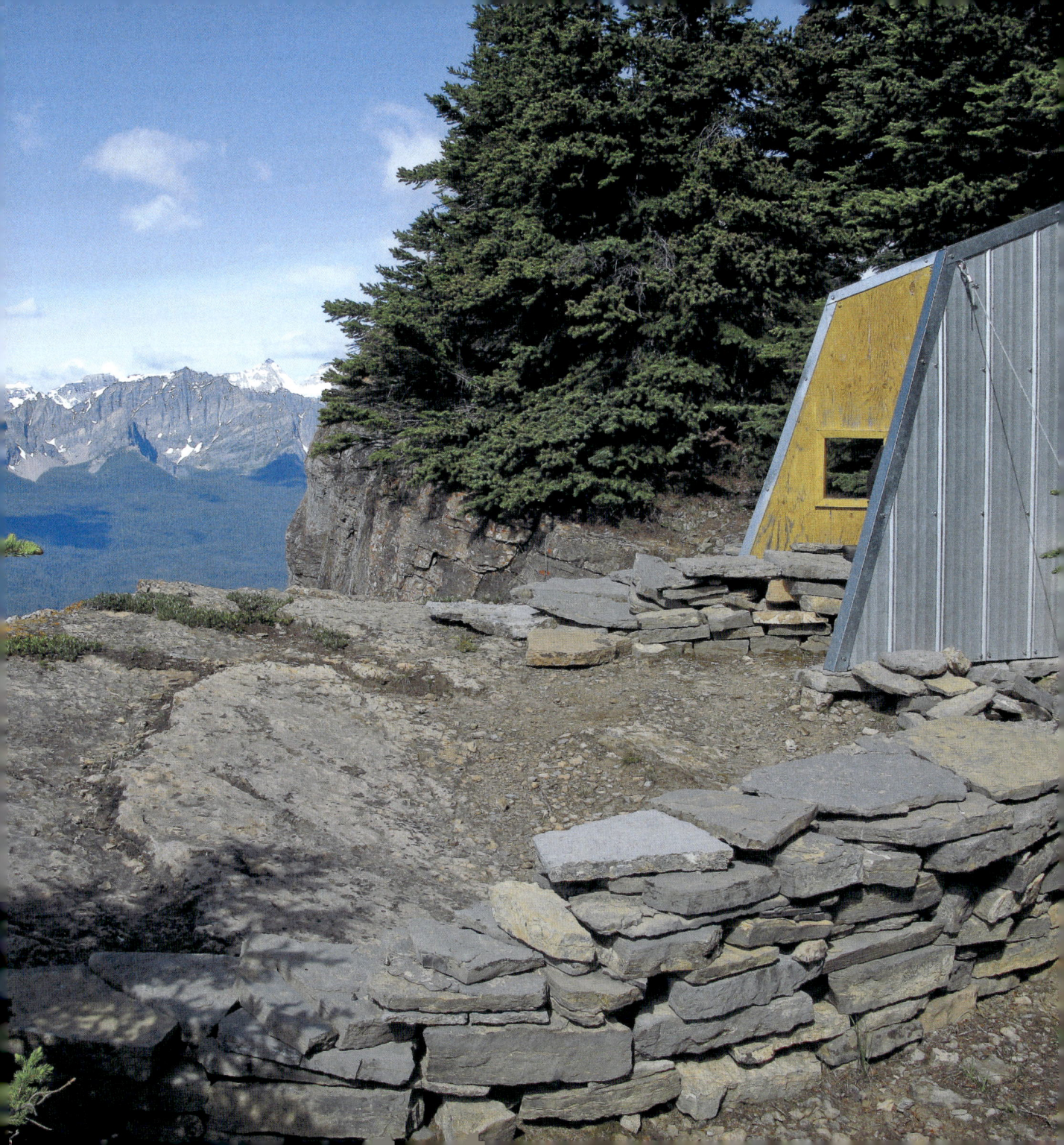

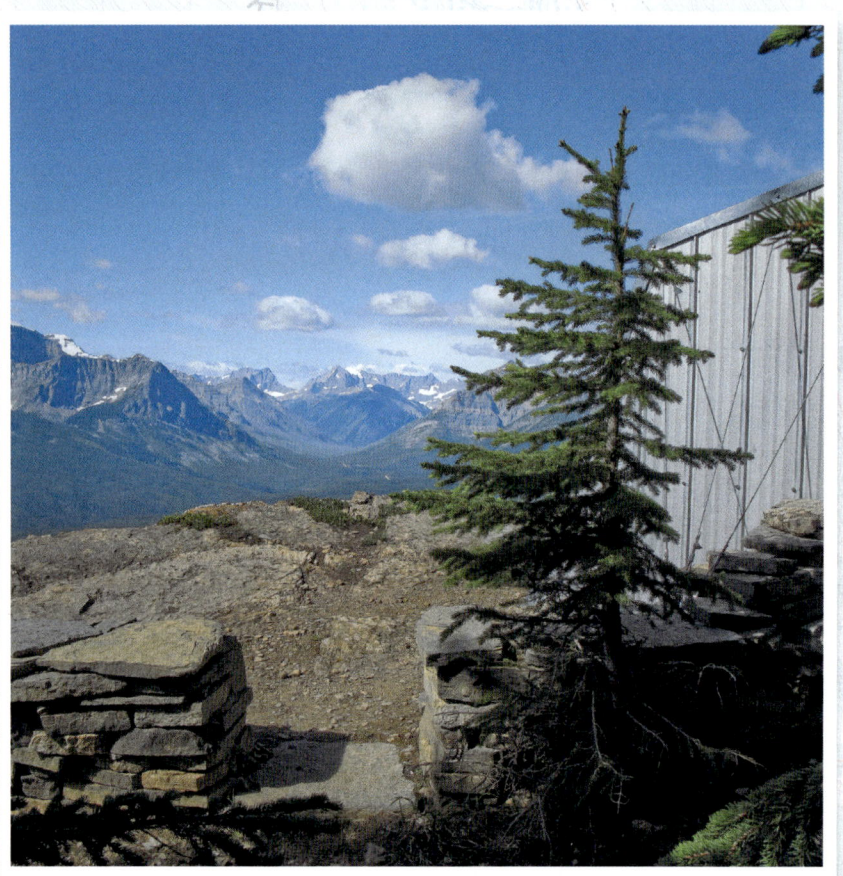

DON'T TRIP GETTING OFF THE CAN!

8 | Poo With a View
Gavin T Boutet

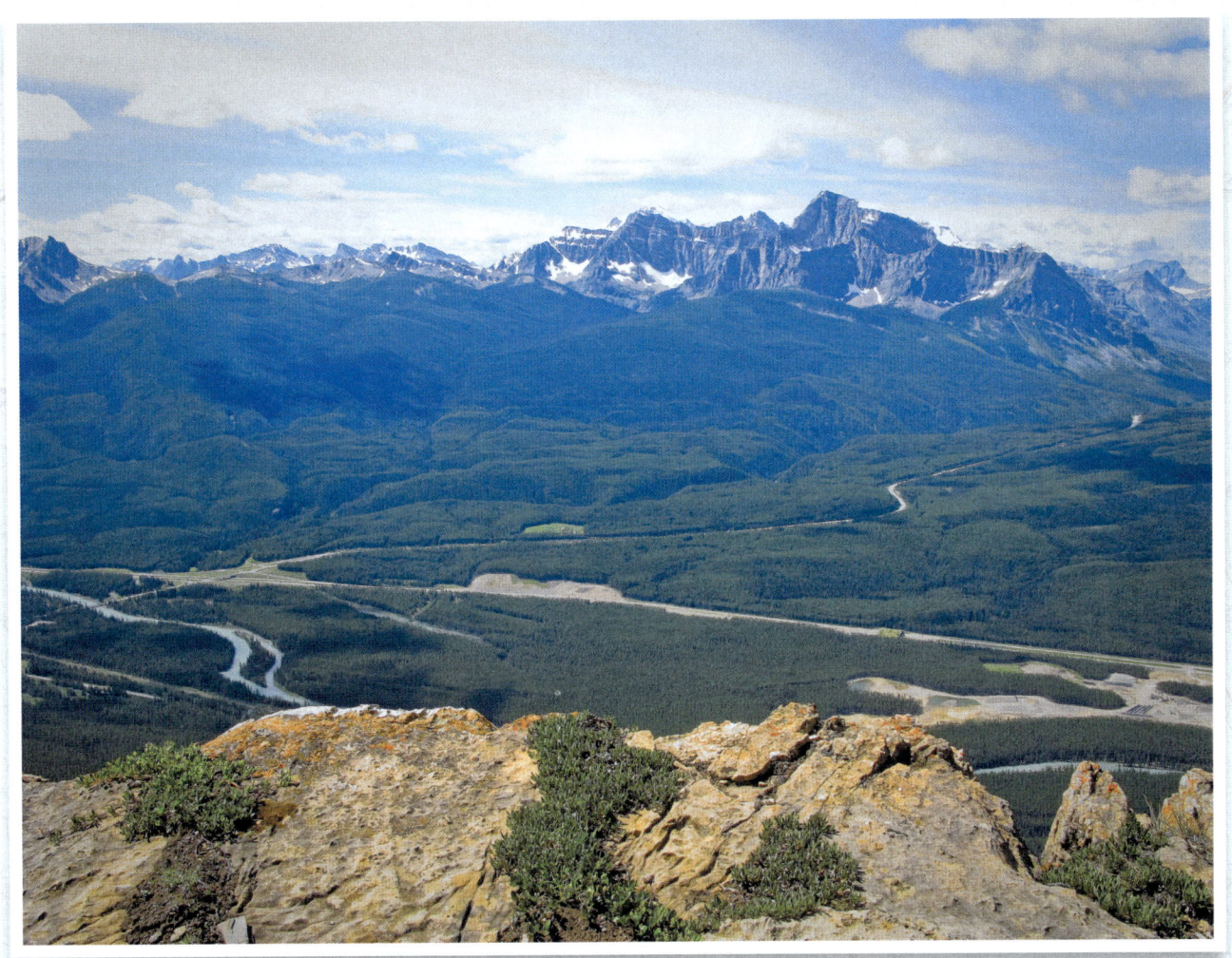

Poo With a View
Gavin T Boutet

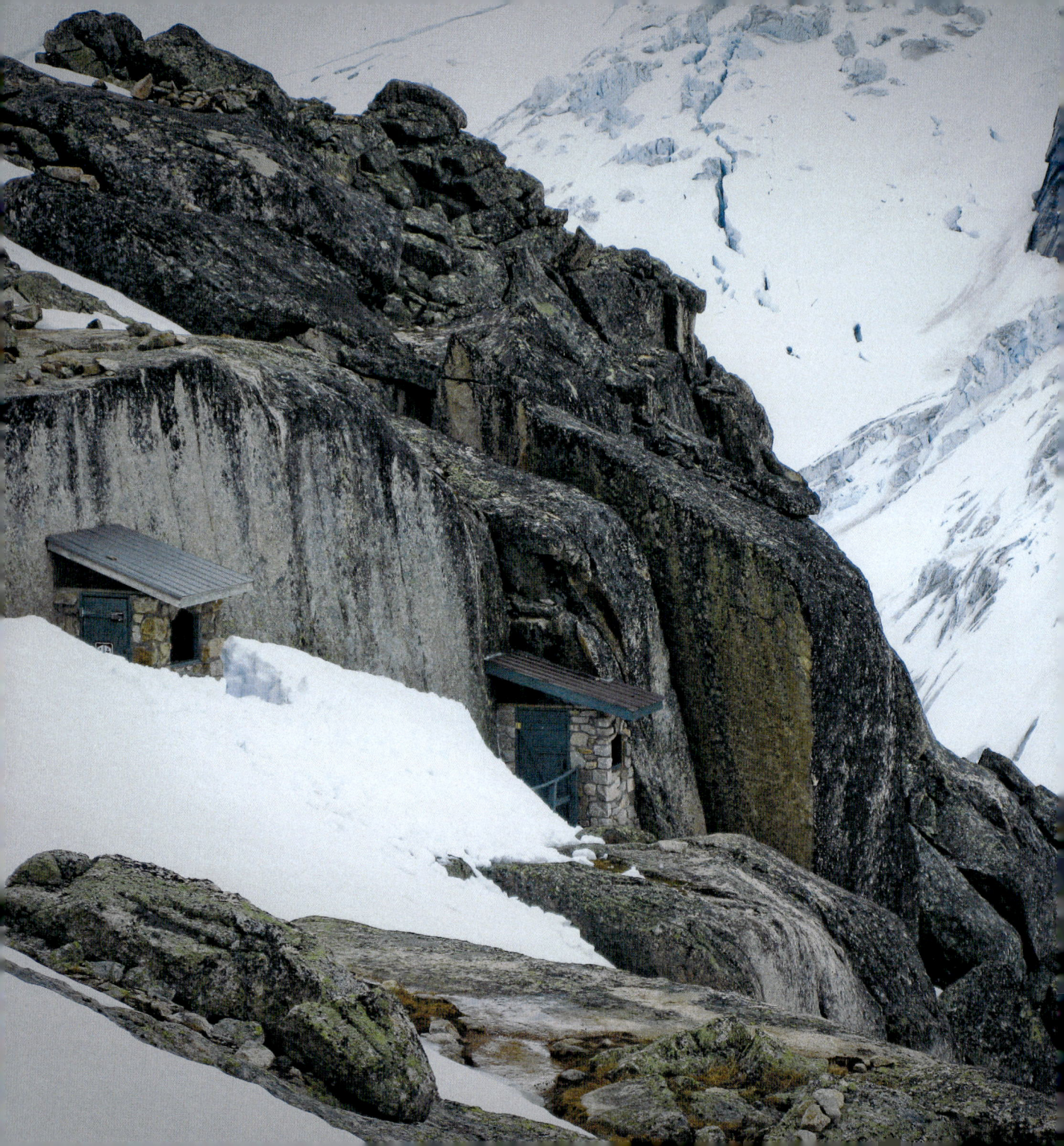

APPLEBEE DOME

2,470 m (8,103 ft)
Bugaboo Provincial Park, British Columbia

Located in the Purcell Mountain range, these privy walls are made from locally sourced rock. Catering to thousands of rock climbers and mountaineers throughout the short summer months, these toilets serve as the alpine base camp for the park.

Poo With a View
Gavin T Boutet

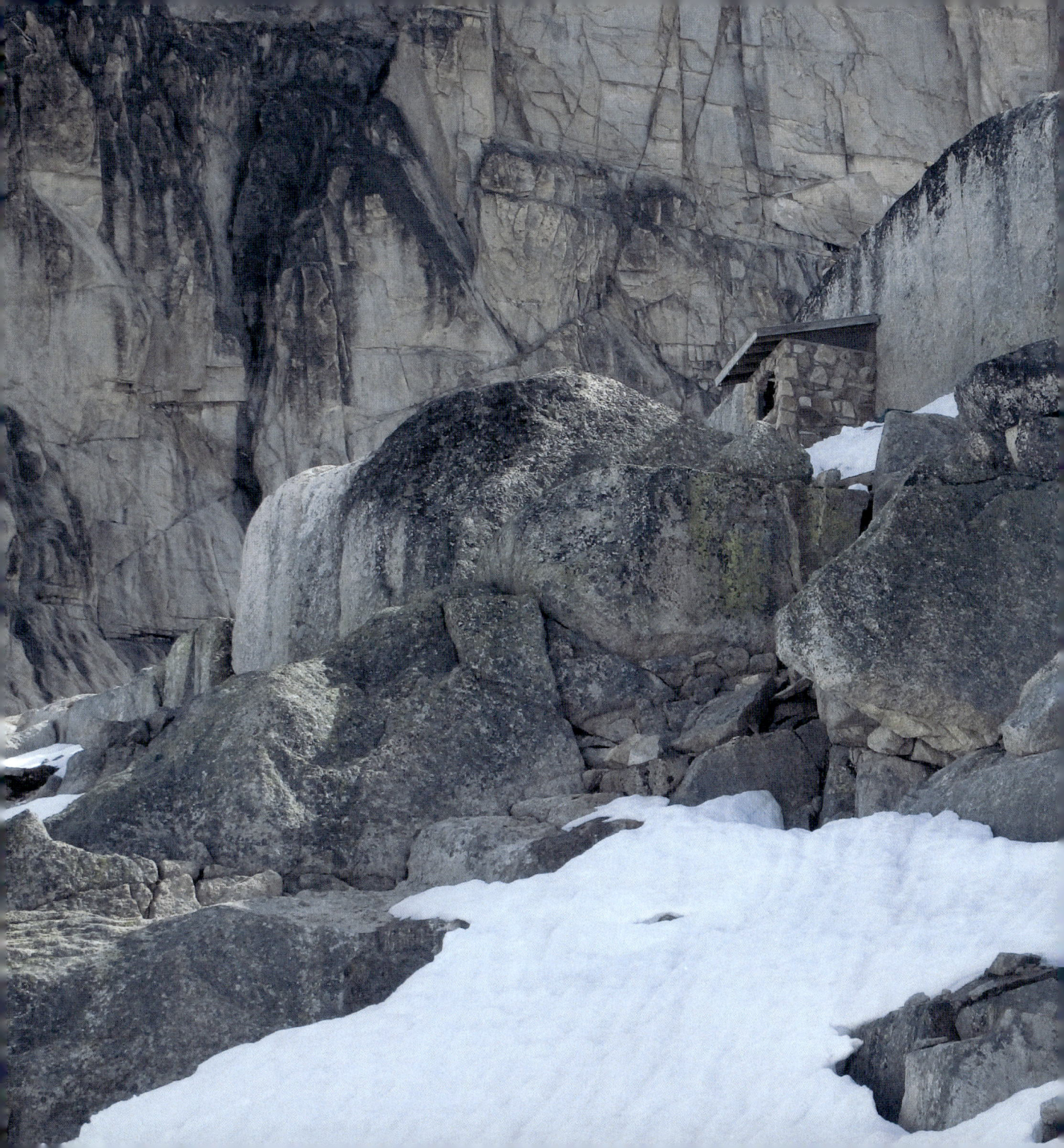

ABBOT PASS HUT

2,926 m (9,600 ft)
Alberta/British Columbia border in Banff/Yoho National Parks

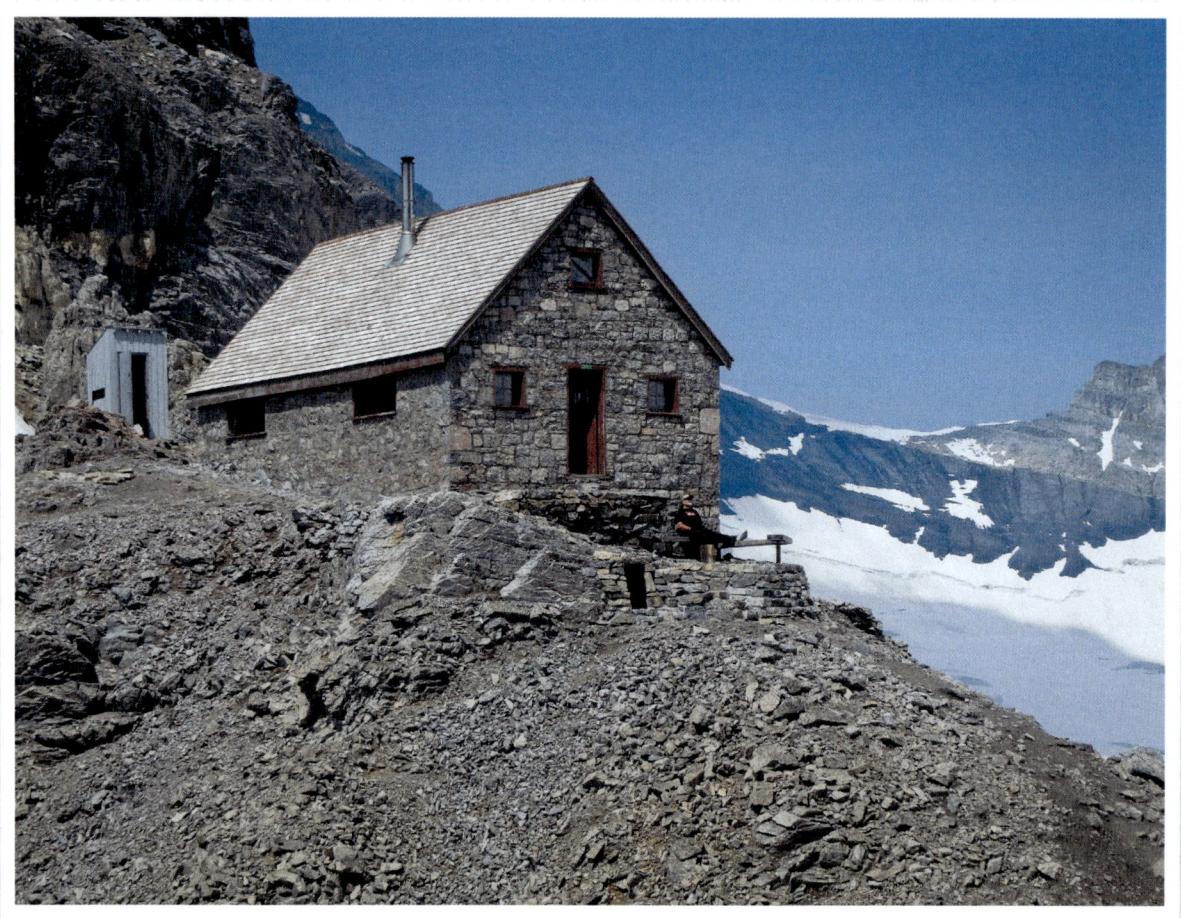

Poo With a View
Gavin T Boutet

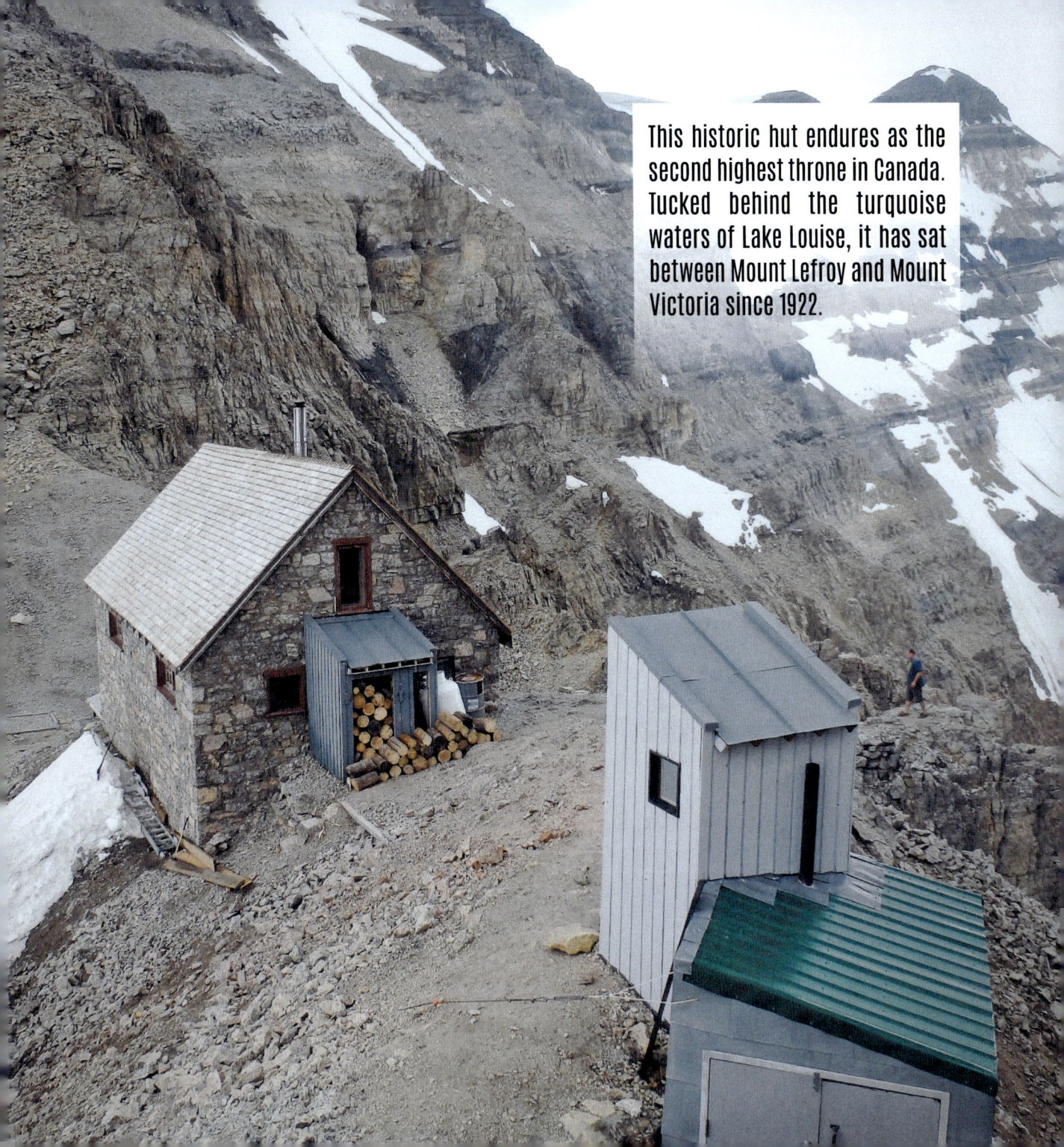

This historic hut endures as the second highest throne in Canada. Tucked behind the turquoise waters of Lake Louise, it has sat between Mount Lefroy and Mount Victoria since 1922.

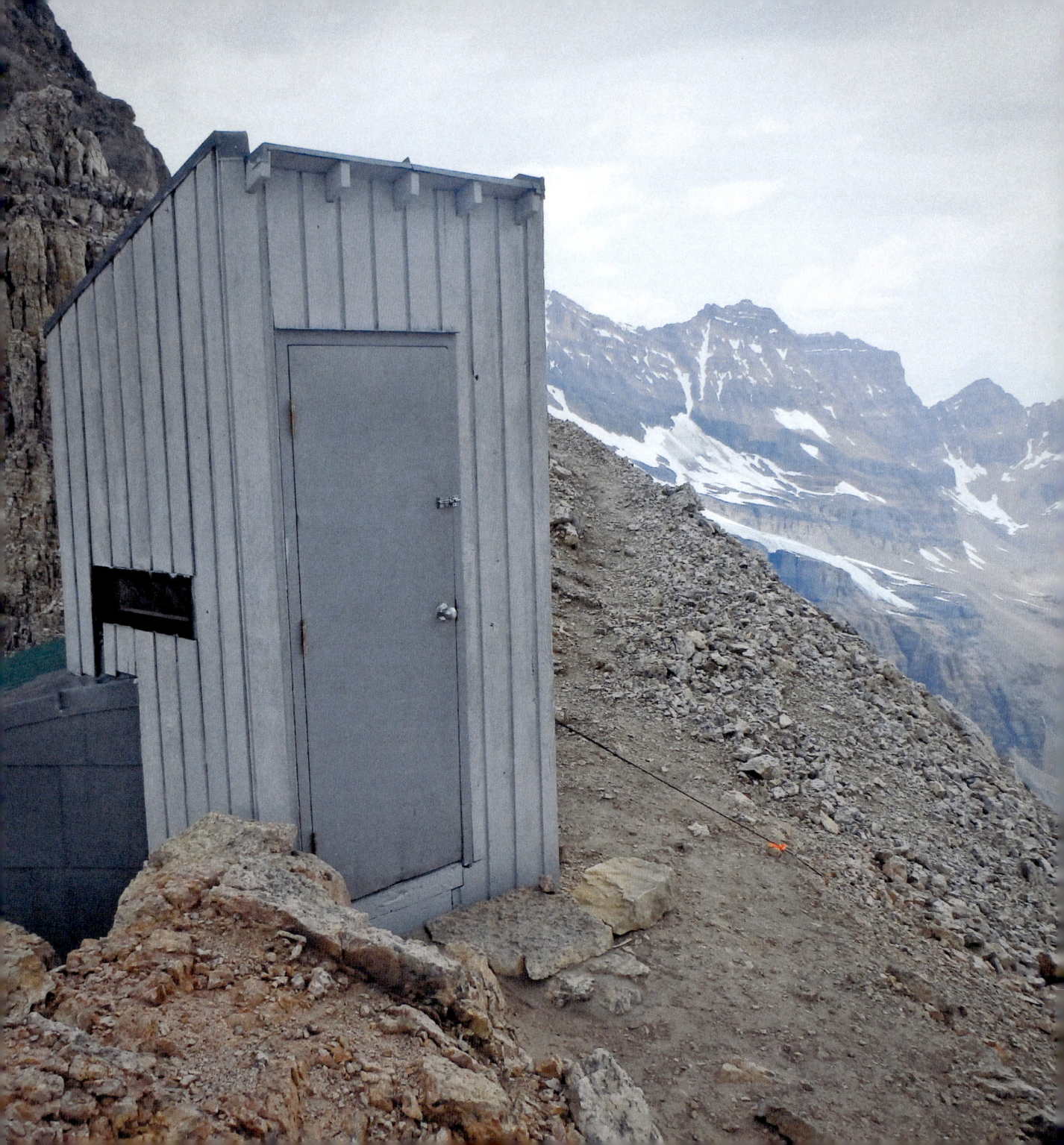

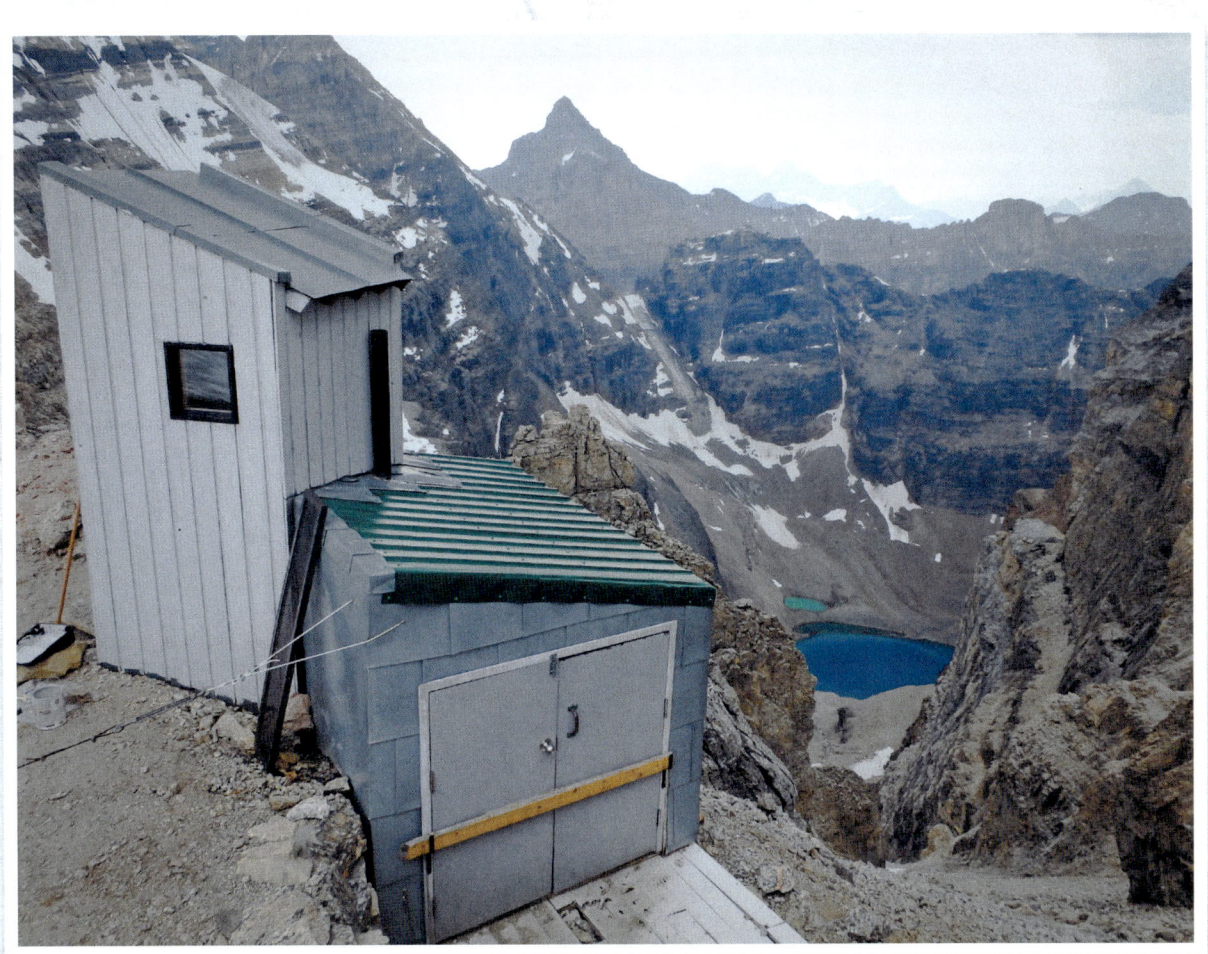

Poo With a View
Gavin T Boutet

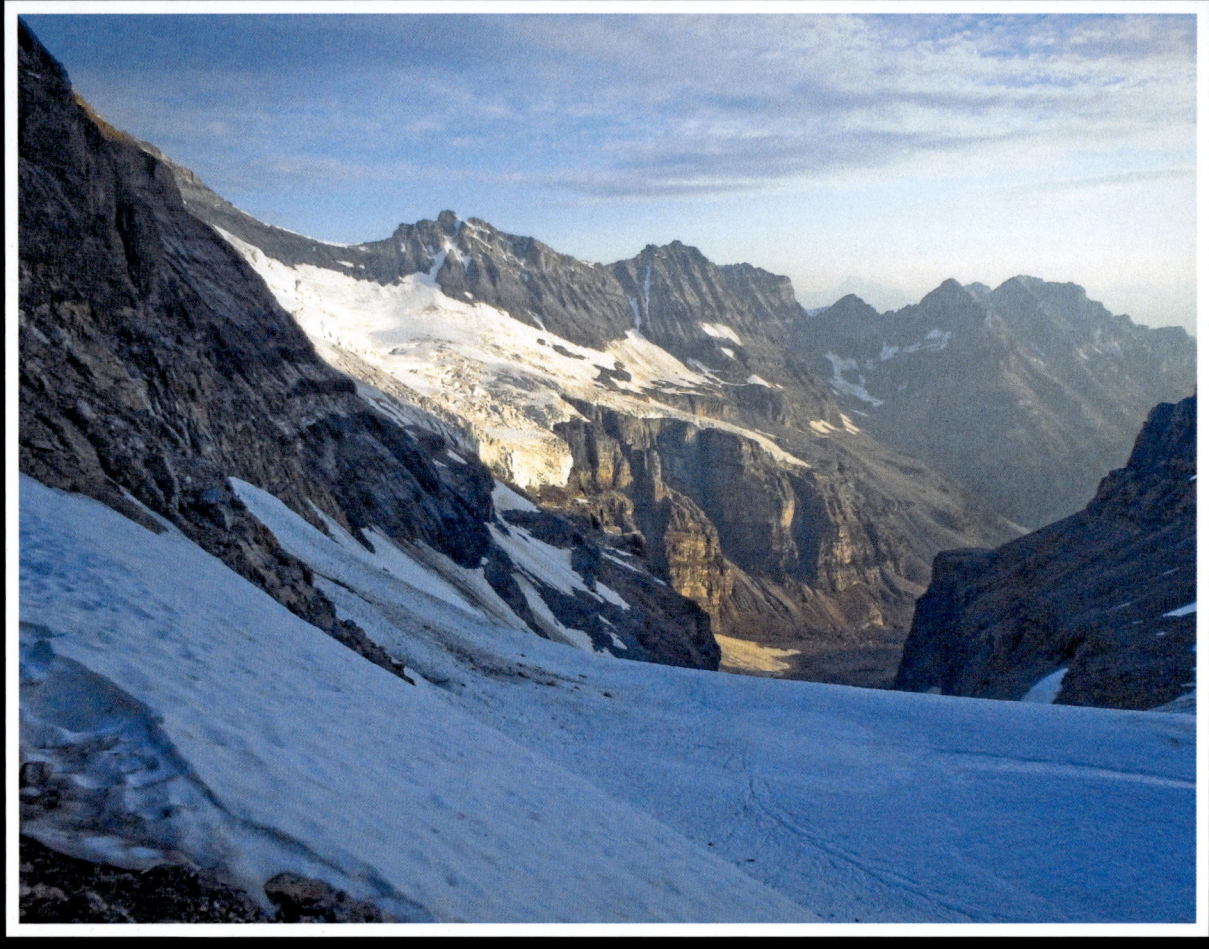

Poo With a View
Gavin J Boutet

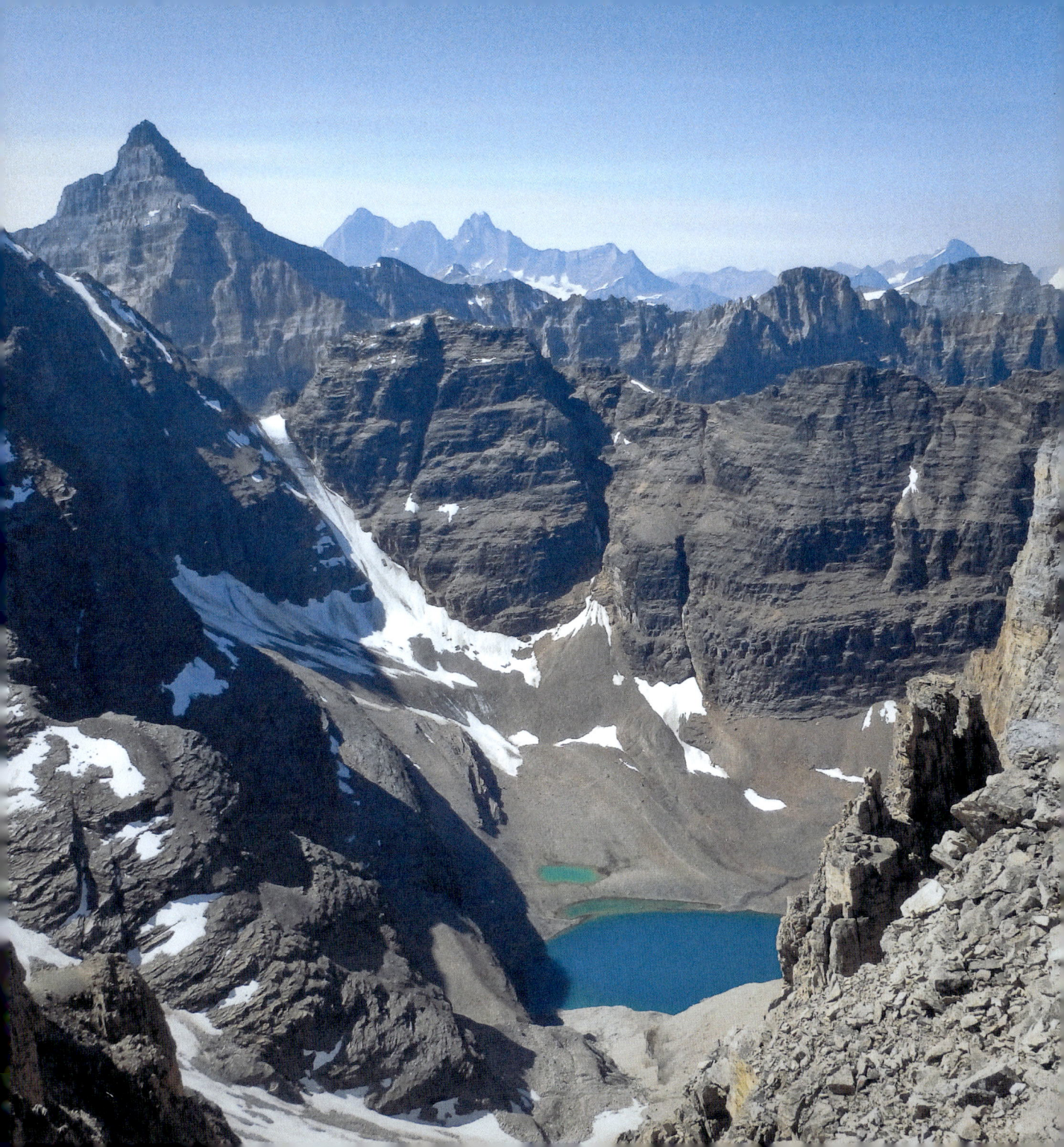

THE WAPTA ICEFIELD

Banff/Yoho National Parks

This stretch of interlinked glaciers north of Lake Louise is heaven for ski-touring enthusiasts and mountaineers alike. A series of huts and their respective johns are a safe haven for experienced travellers and recreationalists looking for an endless winter. Waiting in line at one of these outhouses will ensure a warm seat!

Left top and bottom: Peyto Hut. 2,500 m (8,202 ft)

Top right: Scott Duncan Hut. 2,773 m (9,097 ft)

Bottom right: Ski touring over Bow Glacier.

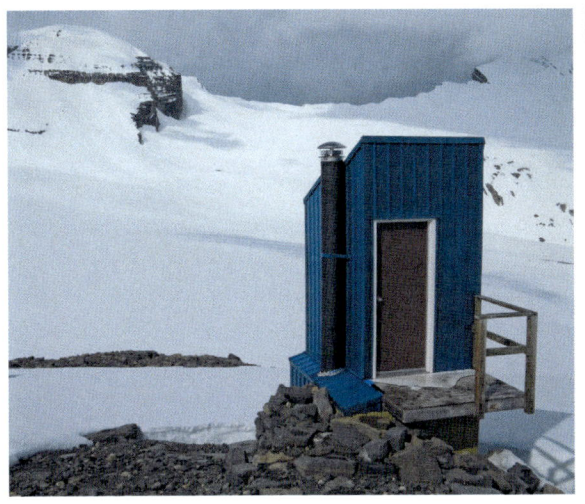
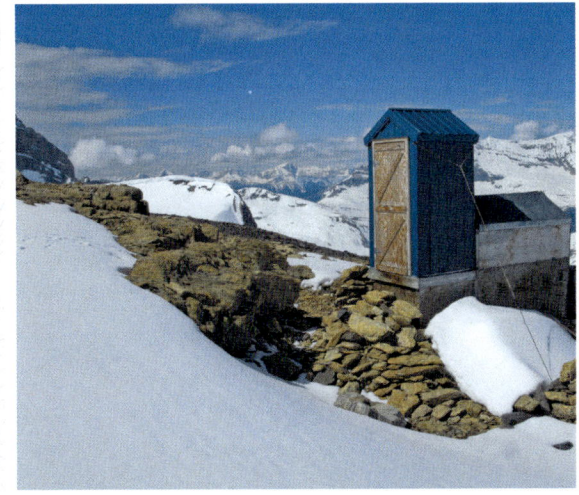
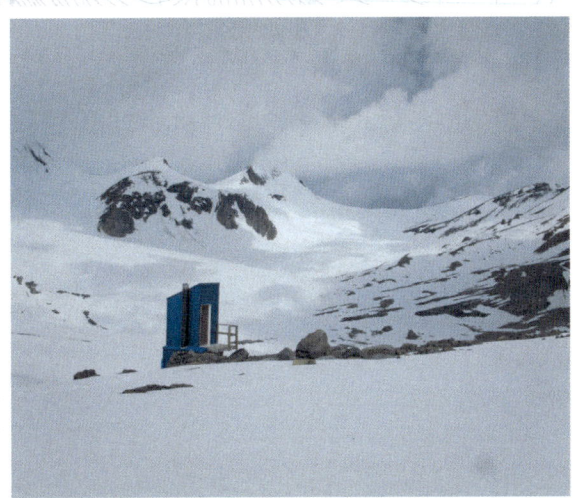
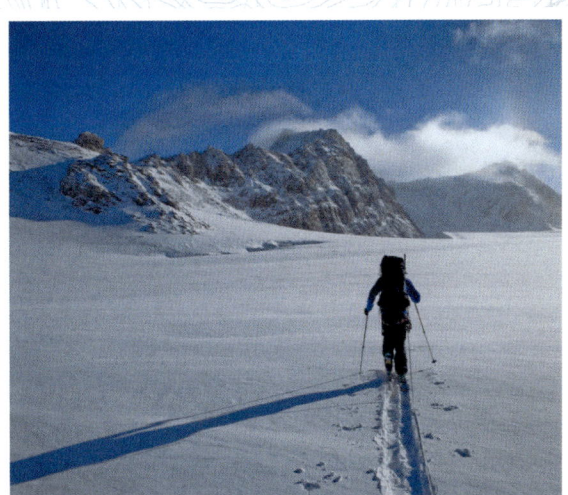

Poo With a View
Gavin T Boutet

CAMP AT DES POILUS

2,585 m (8,480 ft)
Yoho National Park, British Columbia

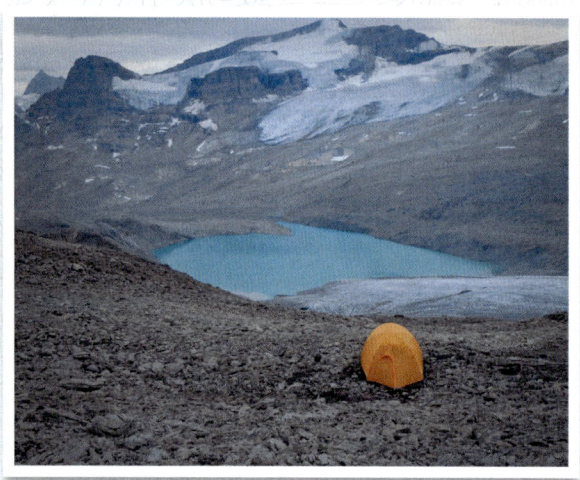 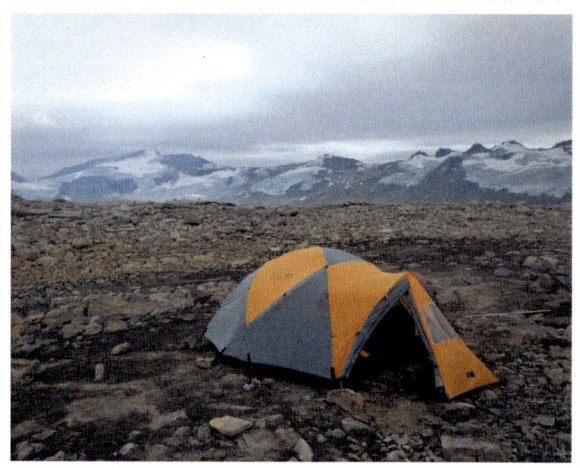

Construction of a new hut along the Wapta Icefield began in the summer of 2015. The work camp was surrounded by incredible views as was the temporary latrine, which brought comforting relief for the crew.

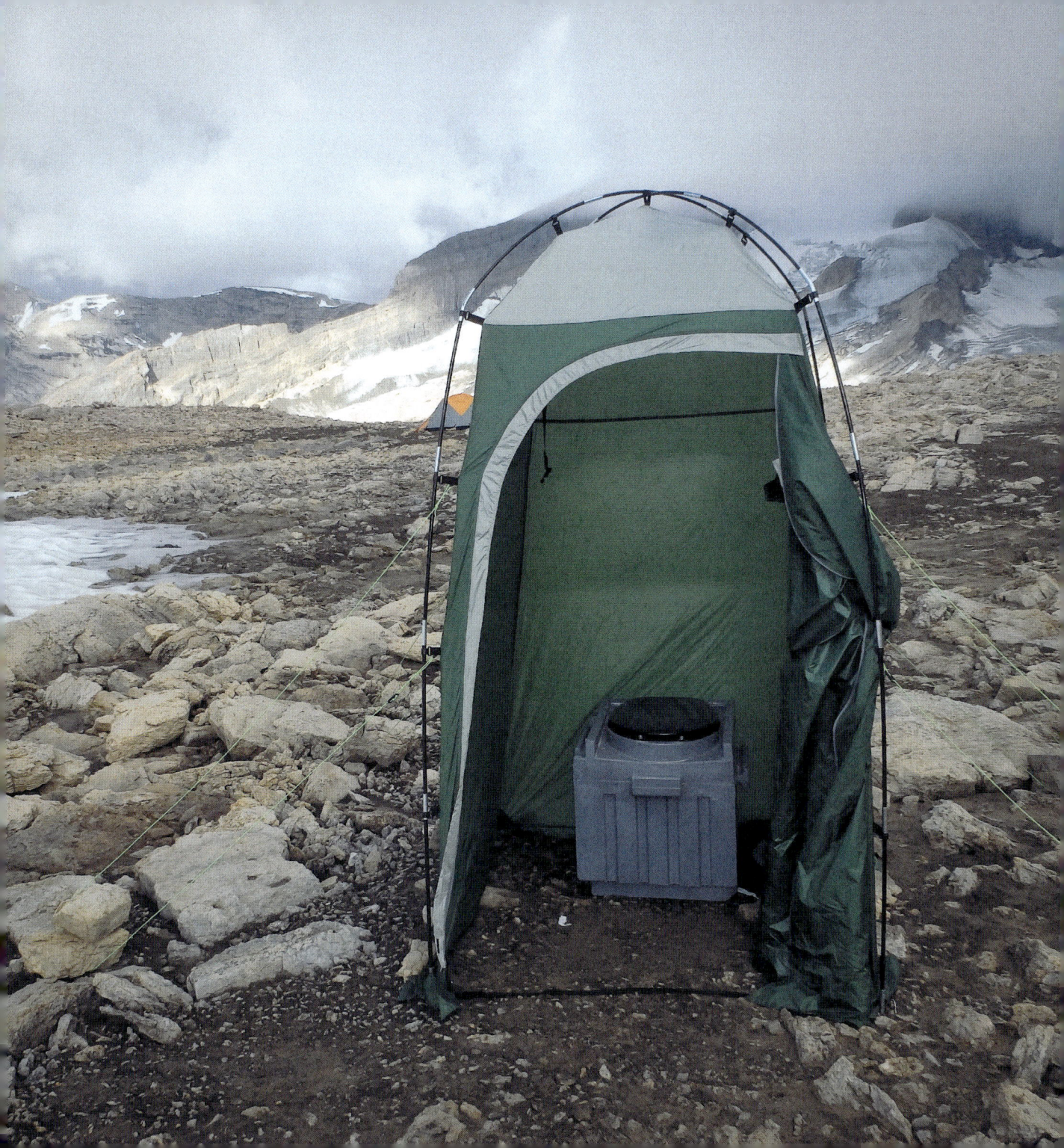

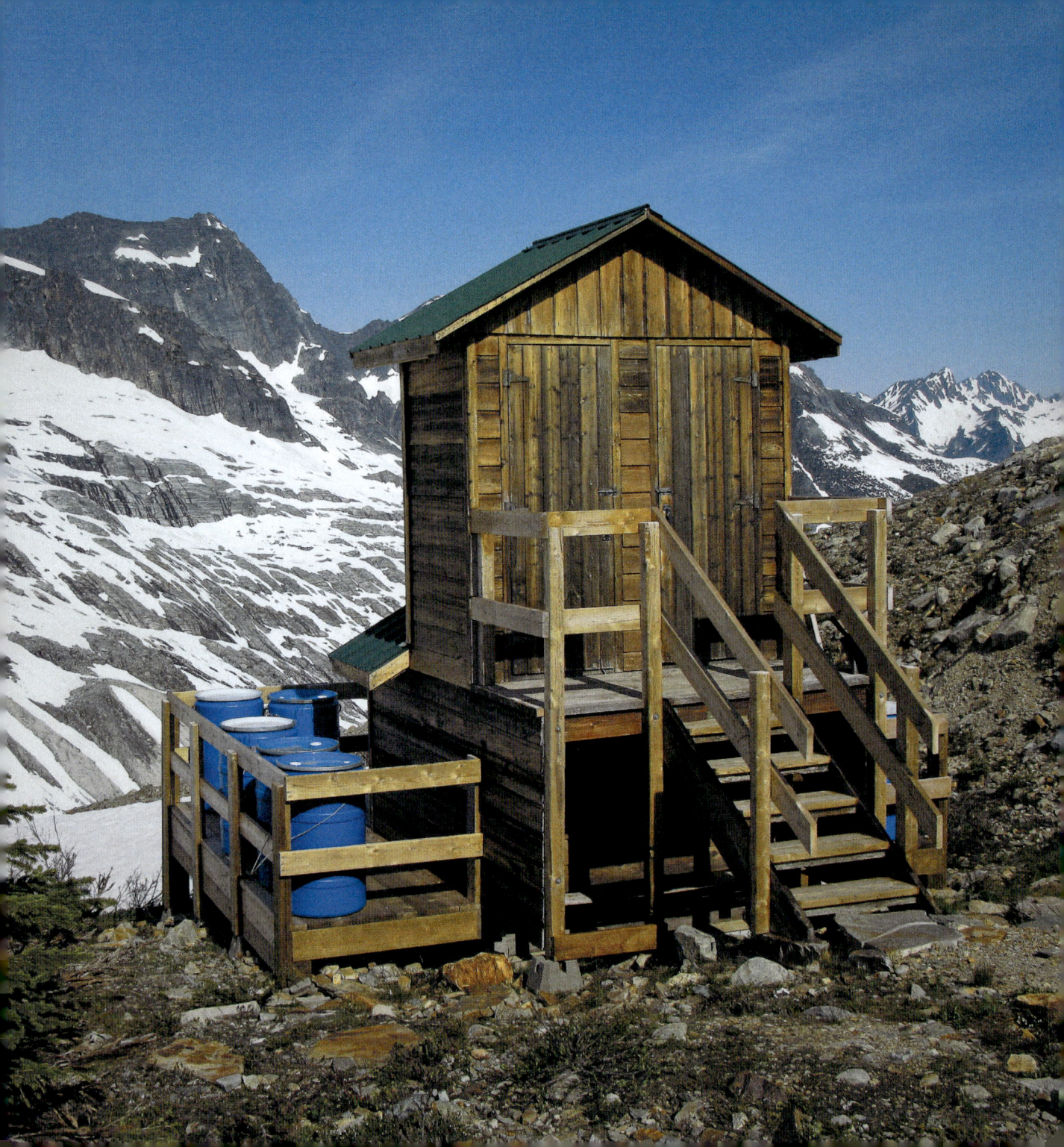

ASULKAN HUT

2,100 m (6,889 ft)
Rogers Pass, Glacier National Park, British Columbia

At the head of the Asulkan Valley lies this wooden loo. It's a comfy seat in the backcountry, and there's even room for two!

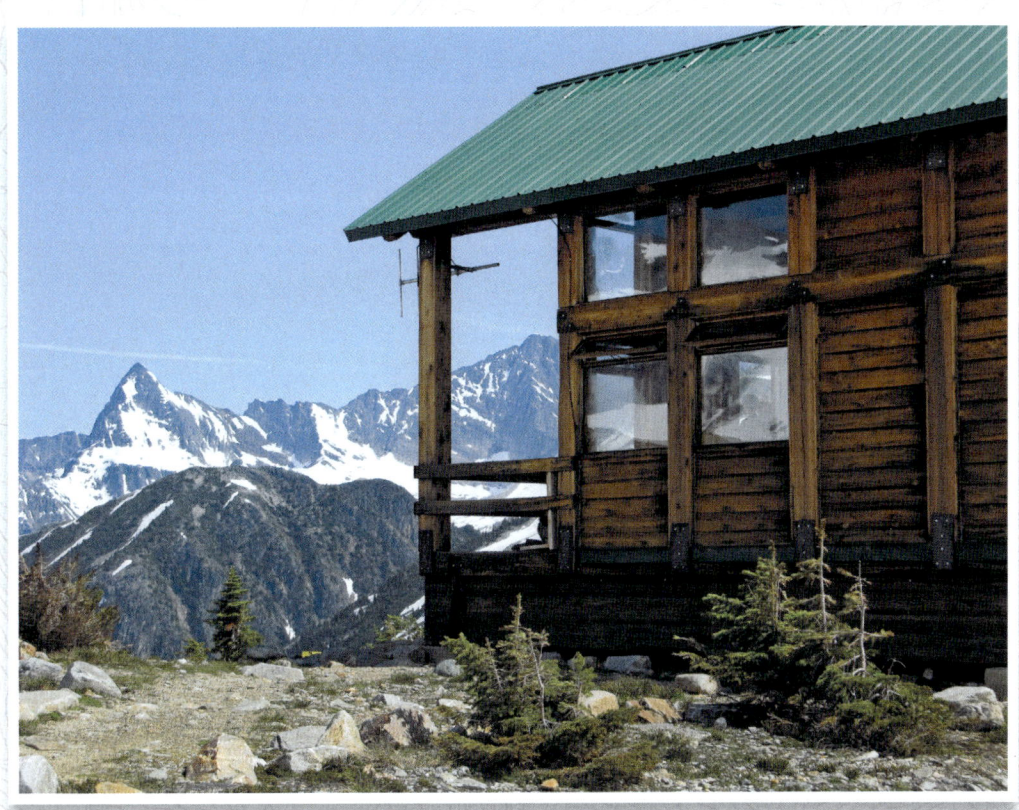

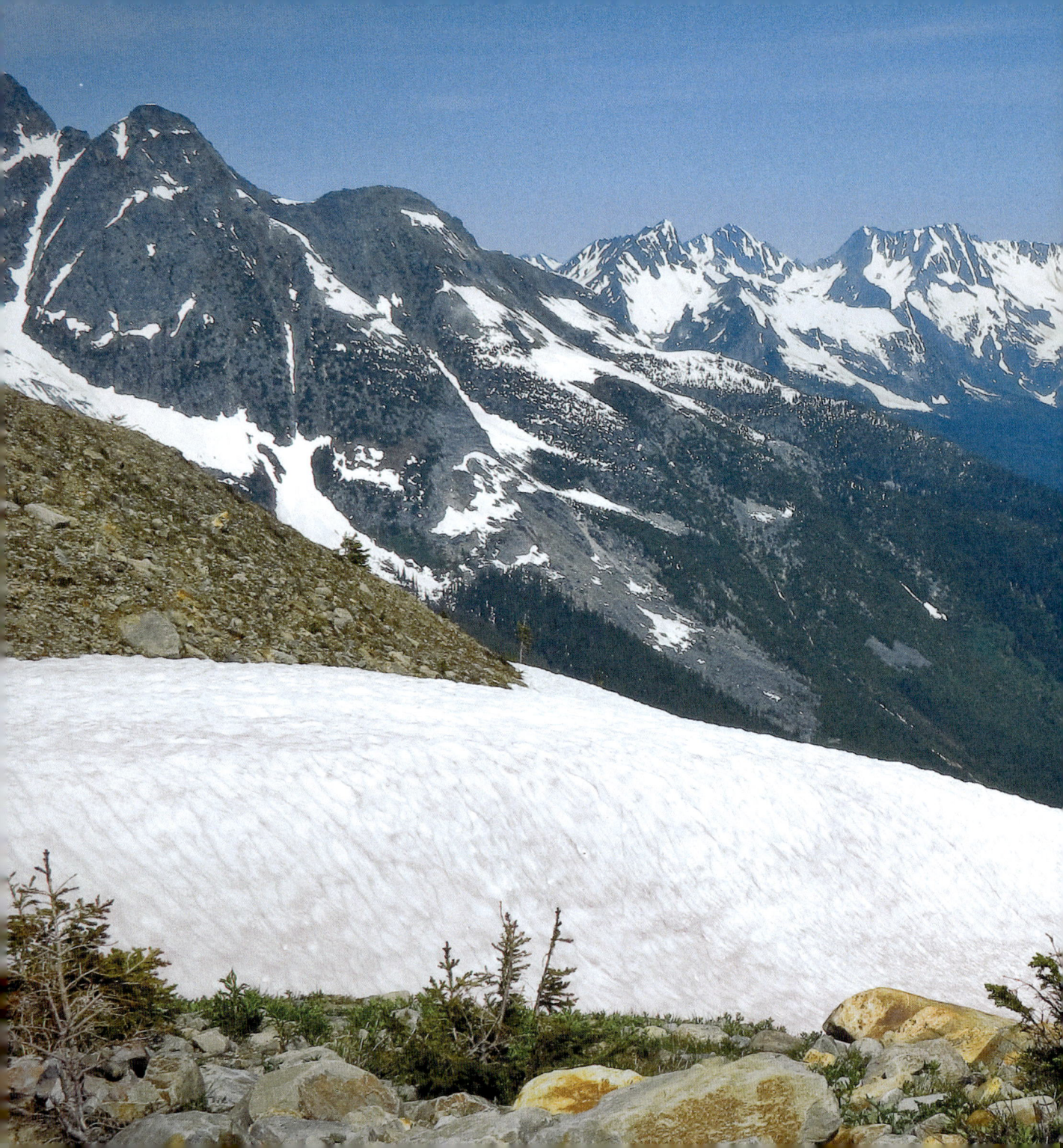

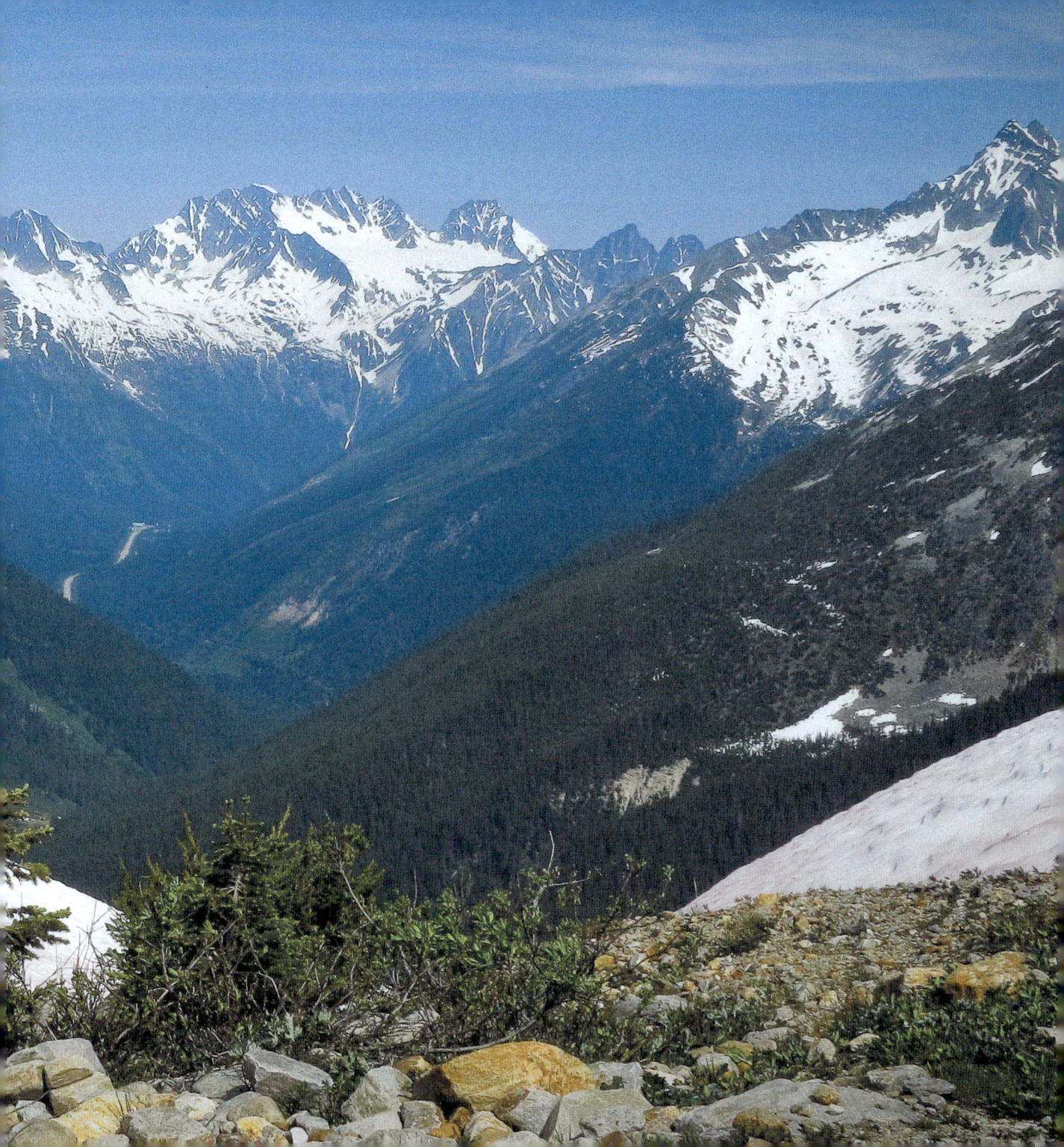

Campbell Icefield Chalet

2,120 m (6,950 ft)
Rocky Mountains, British Columbia

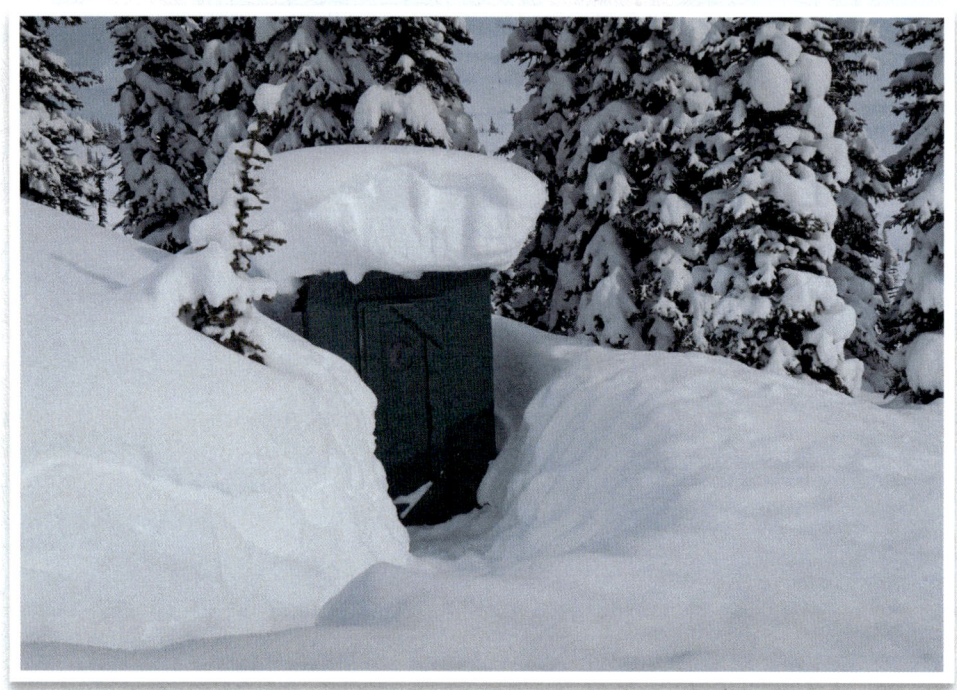

North of Golden, British Columbia, on the snowy slopes of the western Rockies a backcountry gem awaits. When nature calls, the door to this thunderbox should be left open for stellar views of none other than Thunder Mountain.

Poo With a View
Gavin T Boutet

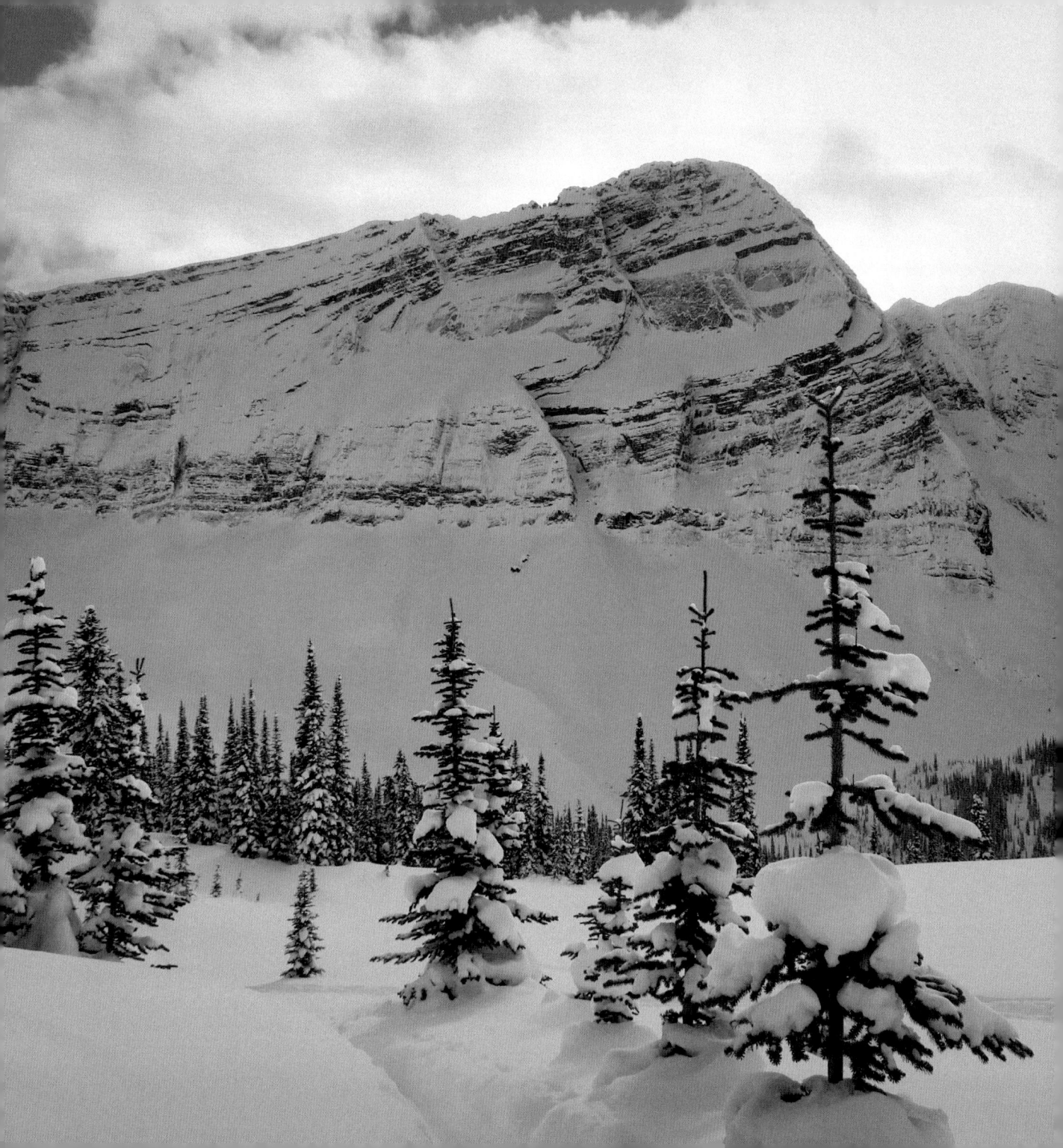

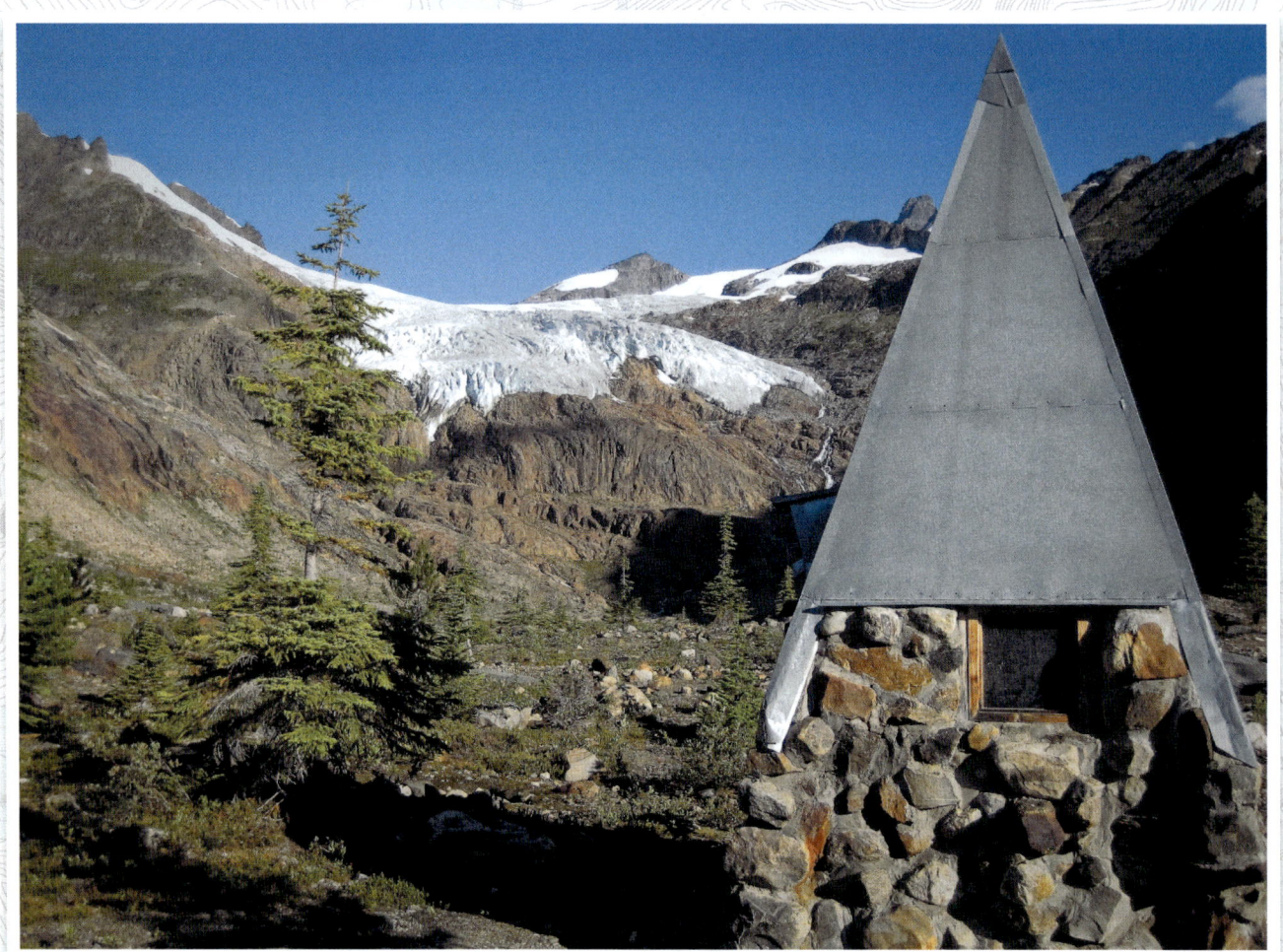

Poo With a View
Gavin T Boutet

GREAT CAIRN HUT

1,890 m (6,200 ft)
Northern Selkirk Mountains, British Columbia

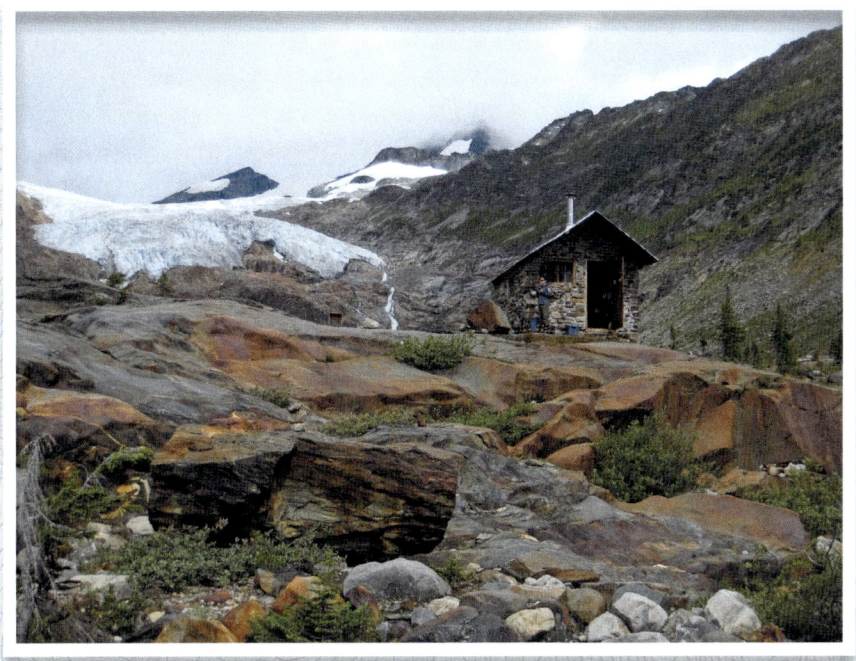

This is the lowest elevation water closet in the book and certainly the most interesting of shapes. This hut and odd-looking biffy are built from rocks that were stacked in this location by mountaineers as a route marker, or cairn, that guided climbers to the base of Mount Sir Sandford.

The cairn potty stands tall amongst the giants!

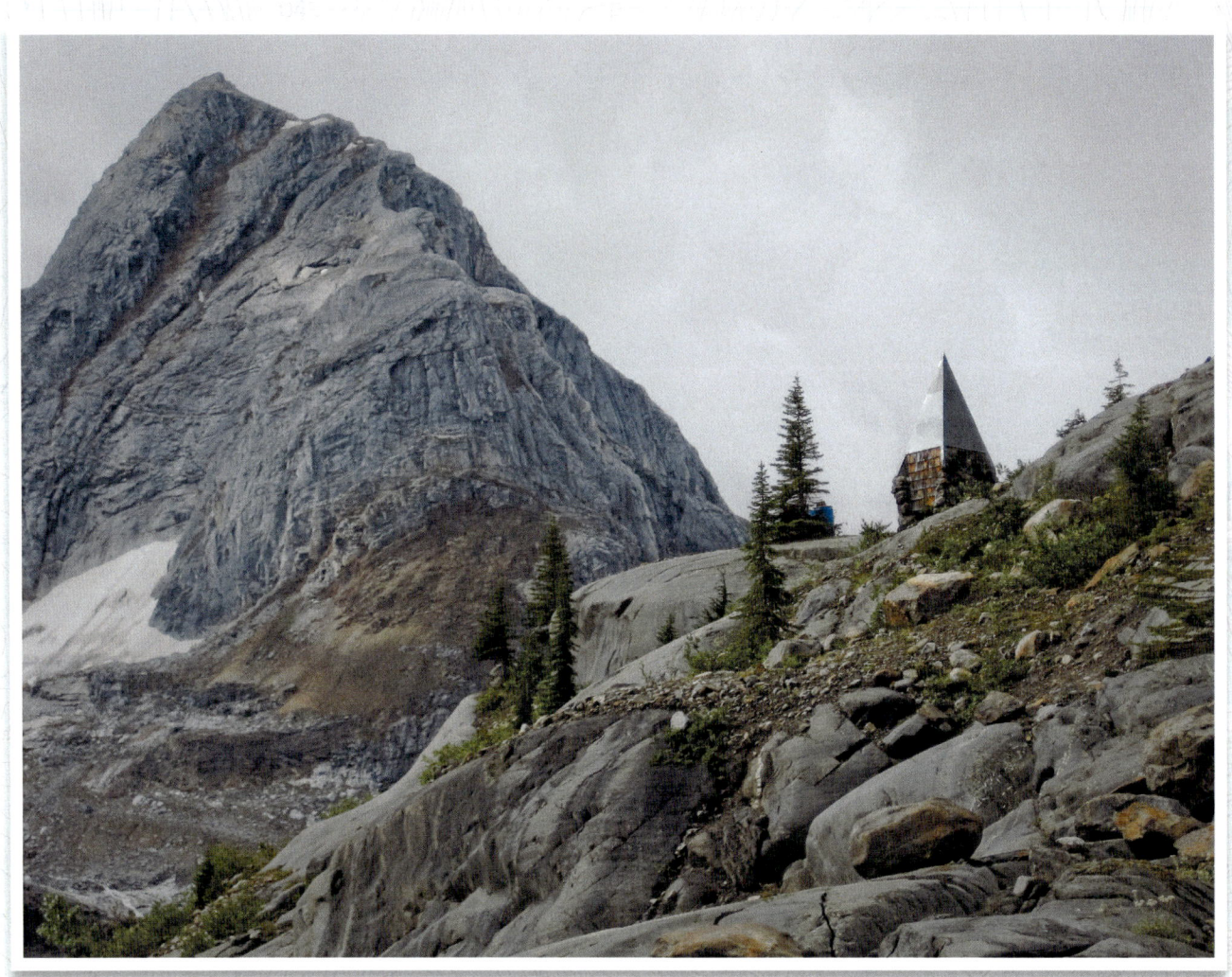

Poo With a View
Gavin T Boutet

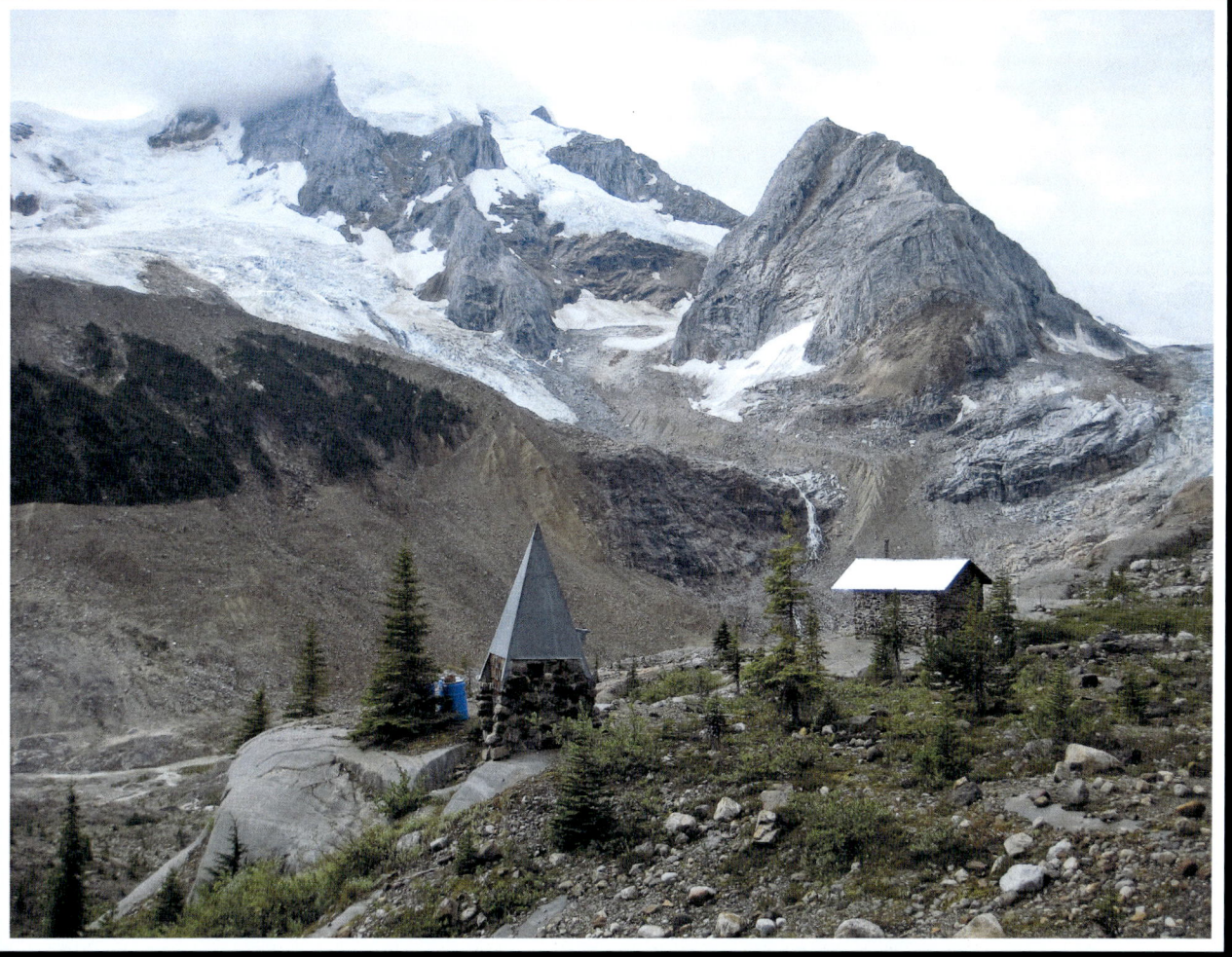

Poo With a View
Gavin T Boutet

PIGEON COL

Elevation unknown - don't look down

Bugaboo Provincial Park, British Columbia

This is a true "open-air" experience clinging to the edge of the world! Built to reduce human impact in a fragile mountain environment, this facility is in a location not for the faint-hearted. It's a commode in a tight spot for the kings and queens of the mountains.

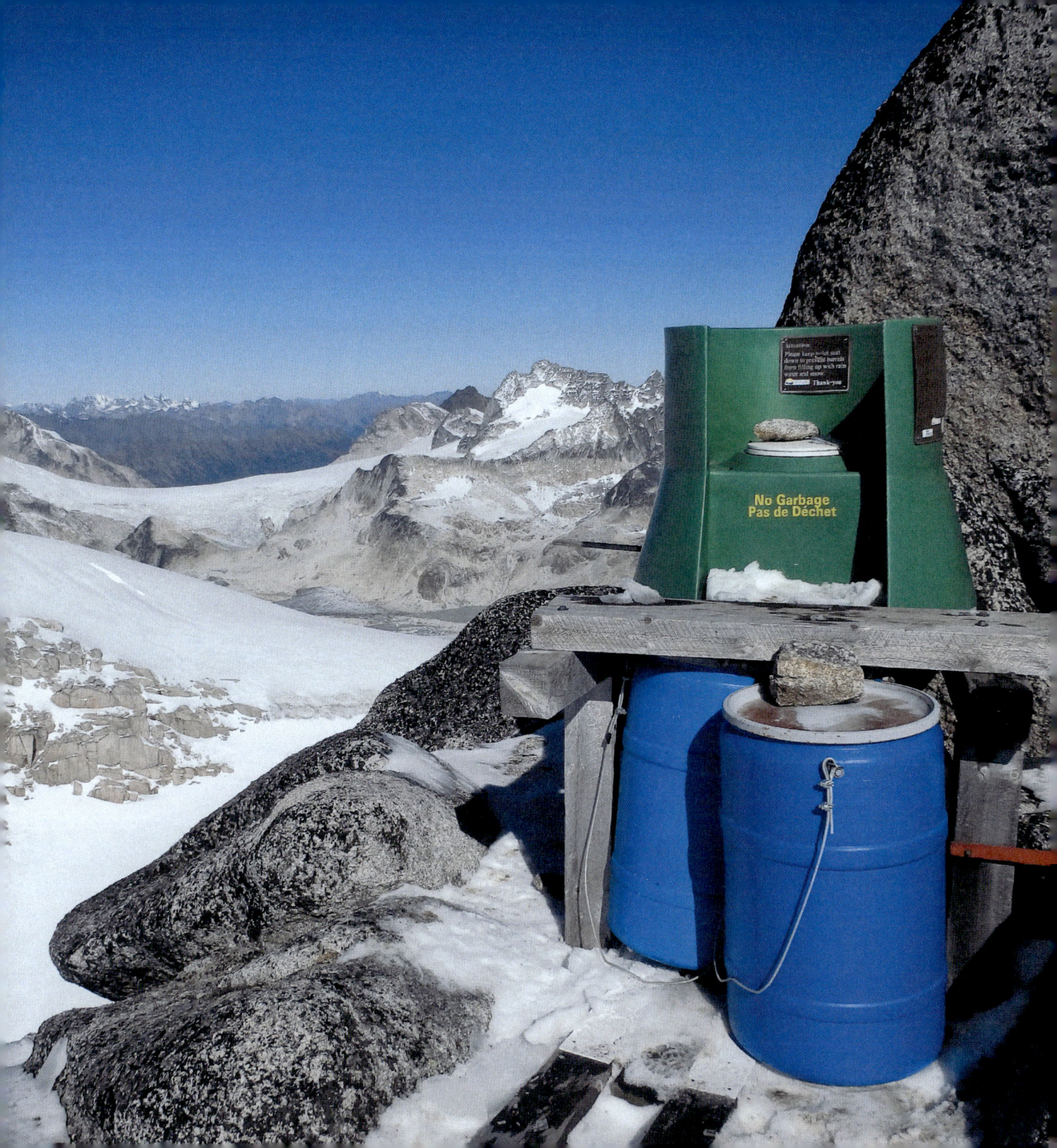

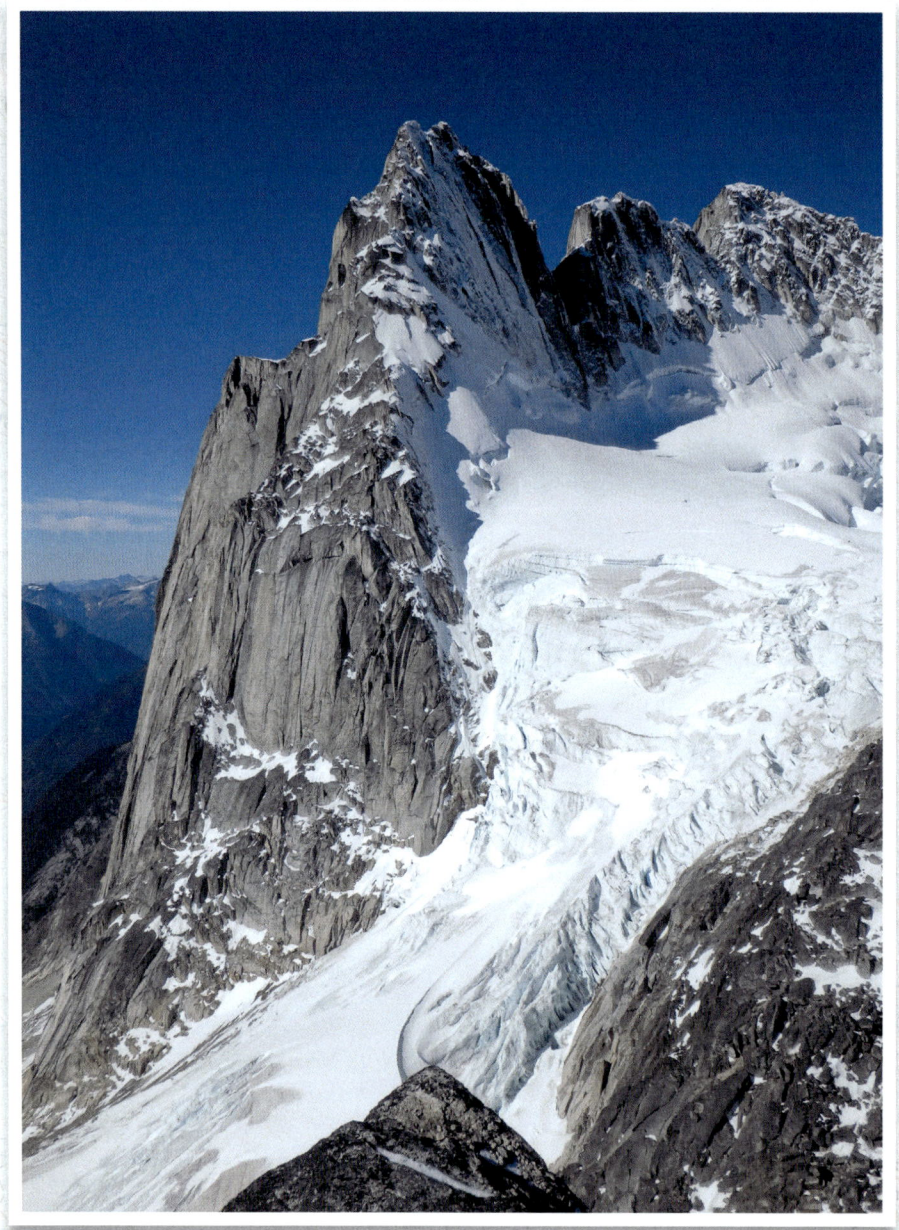

Poo With a View
Gavin T Boutet

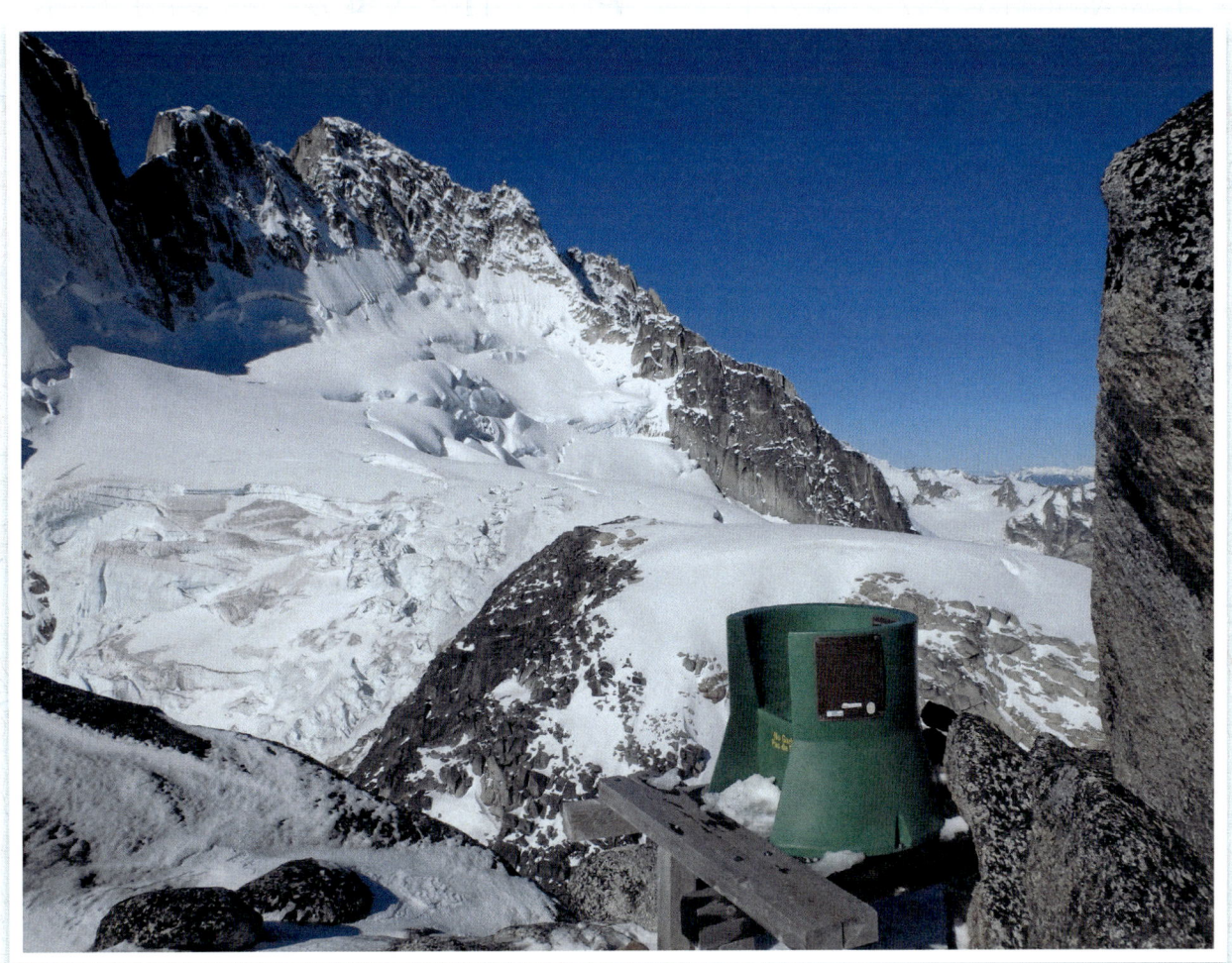

Poo With a View
Gavin T Boutet

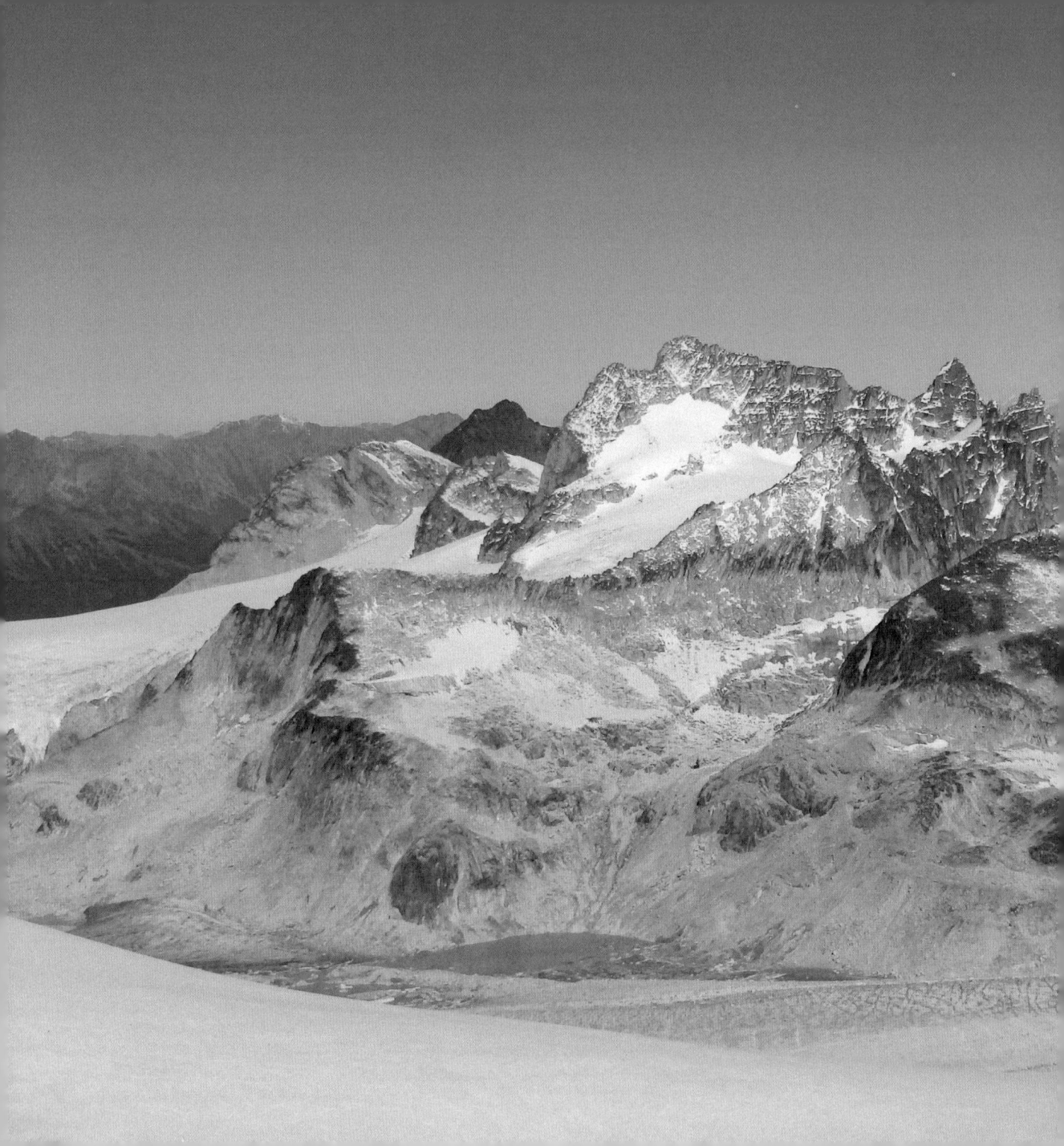

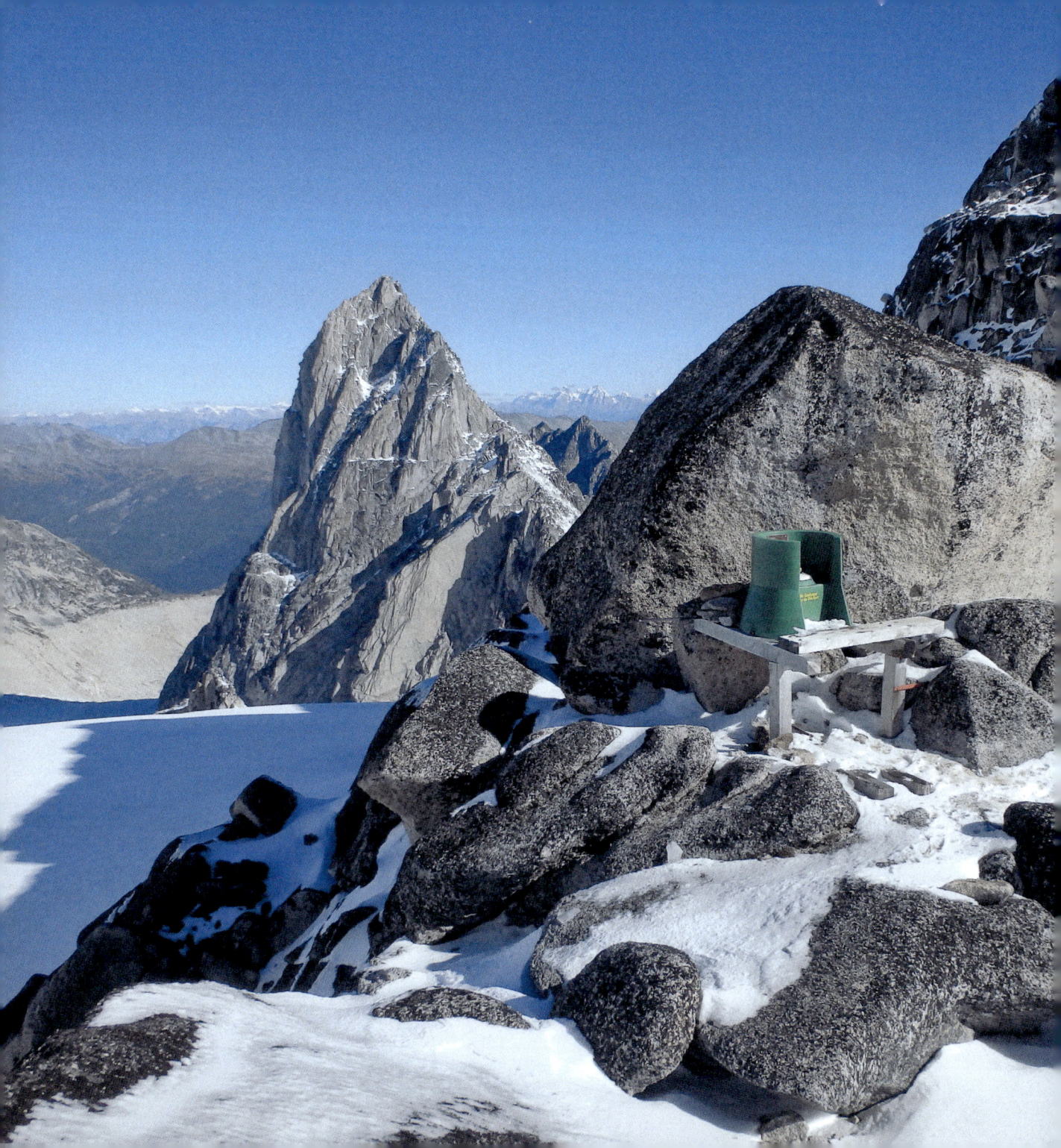

NEIL COLGAN HUT

2,955 m (9,695 ft)
Alberta/British Columbia border in Banff/Kootenay National Parks

This is one of the last photos of the old can before it was torn down and rebuilt beside the hut in 2013. It was the highest permanent shitter in Canada and was drafty to say the least. Wandering off at night was not advised!

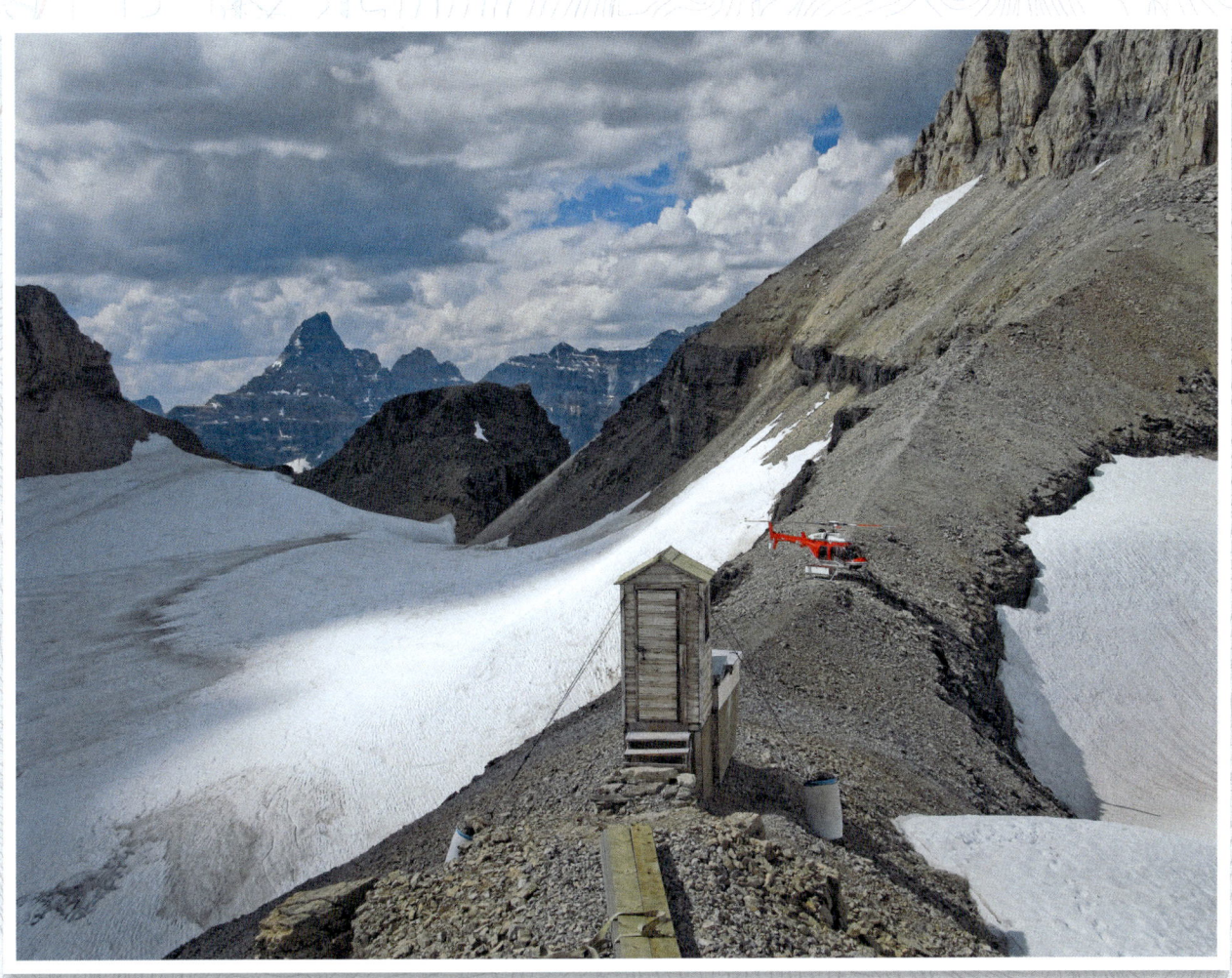

Poo With a View
Gavin T Boutet

BUGABOO – SNOWPATCH COL

Approximately 2,750 m (9,022 ft)
Bugaboo Provincial Park, British Columbia

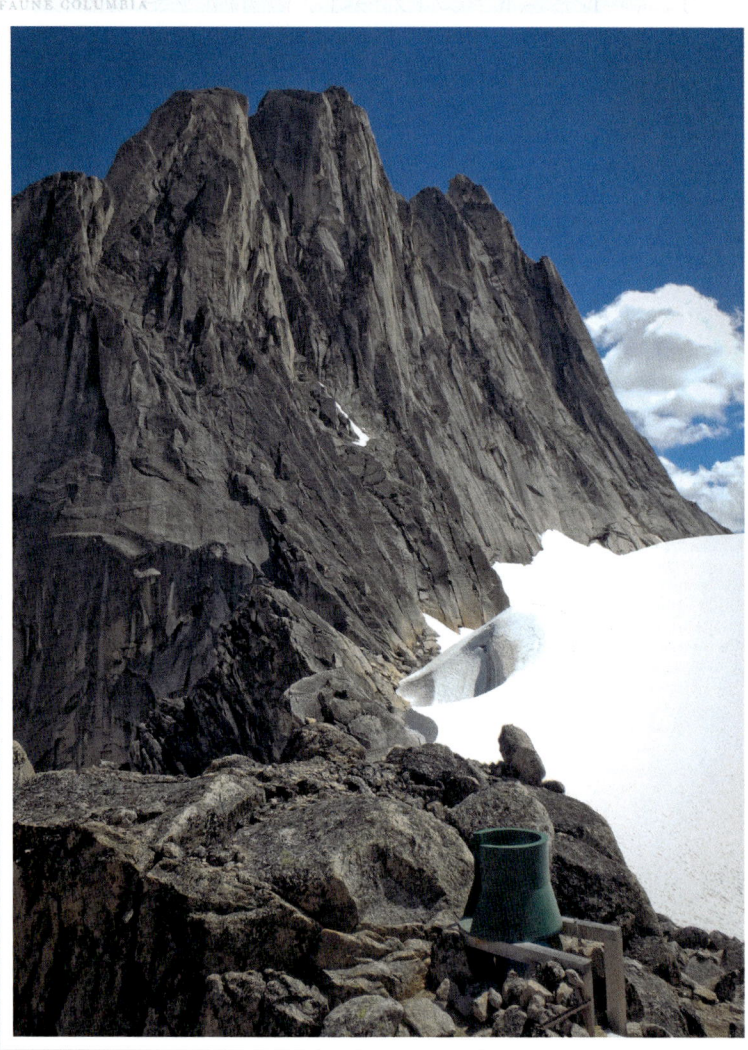

Poo With a View
Gavin T Boutet

Between these two towering peaks lies one of the most scenic and potentially least private crappers in the country. Hopefully, there's no lineup so you can enjoy the incredible view of Snowpatch Spire (left) and Howser Spire (right).

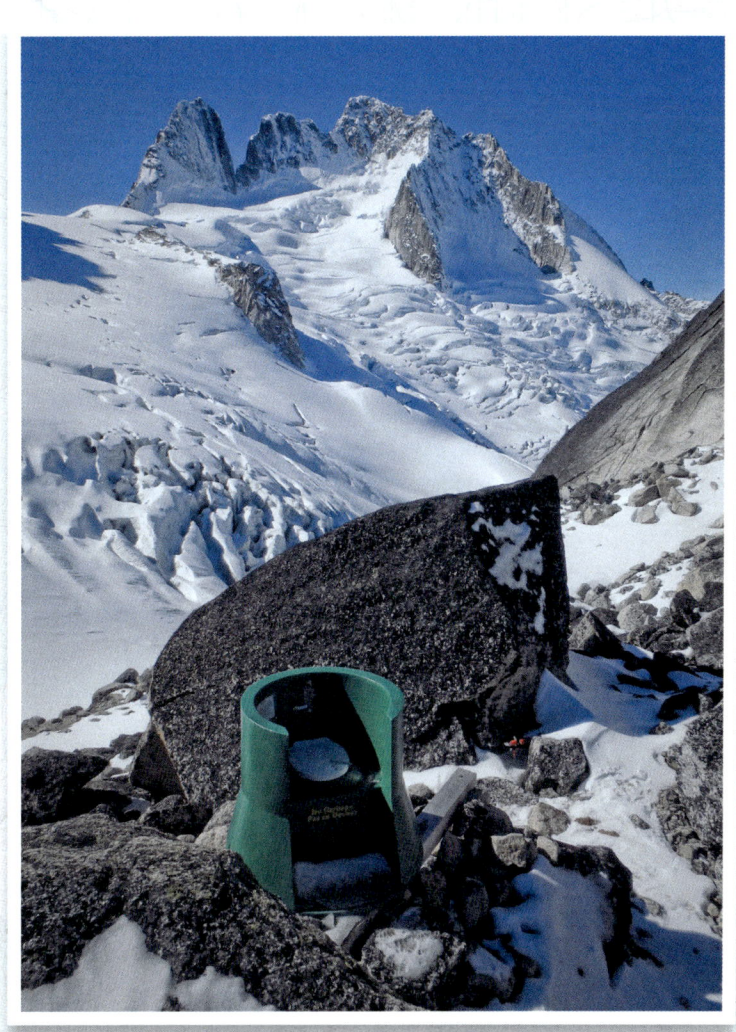

Poo With a View
Gavin T Boutet

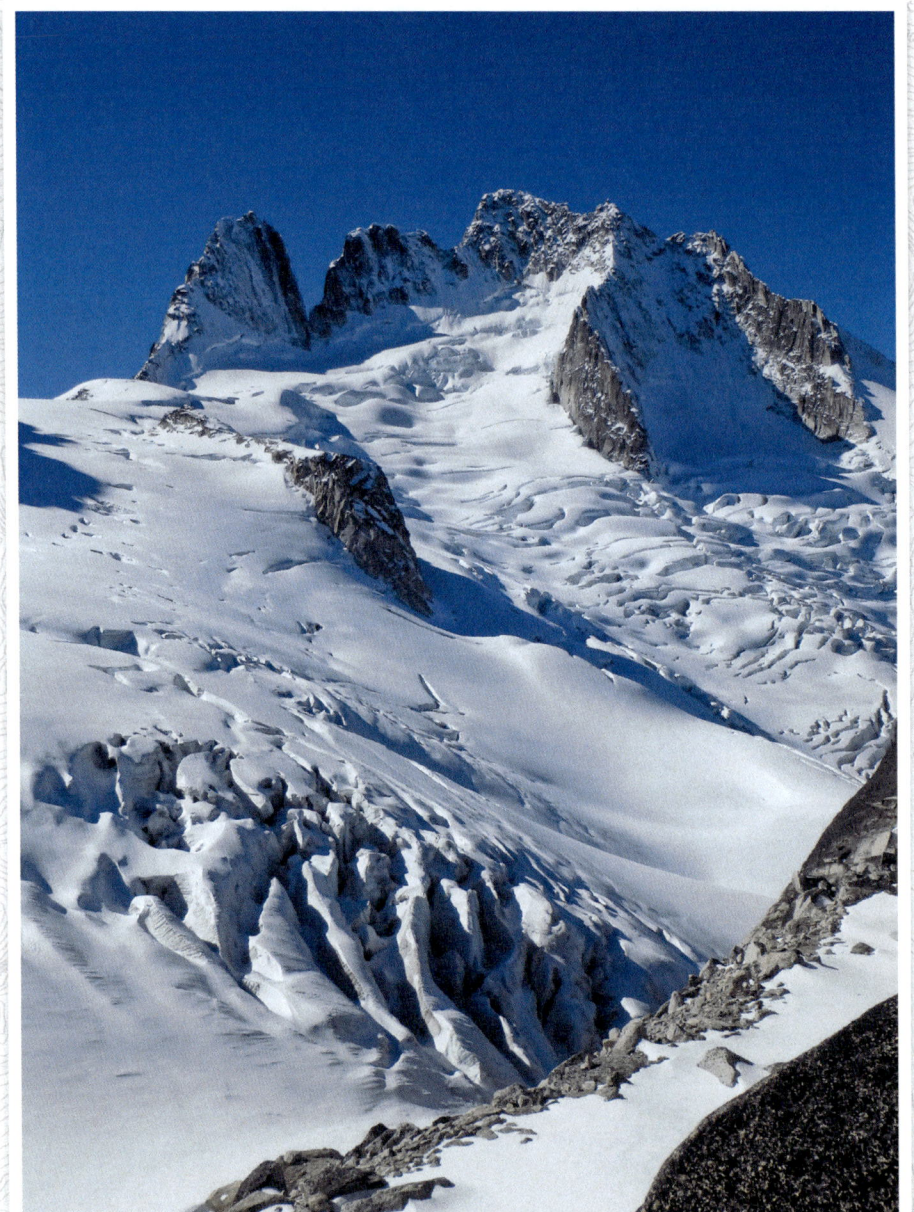

Poo With a View
Gavin T Boutet

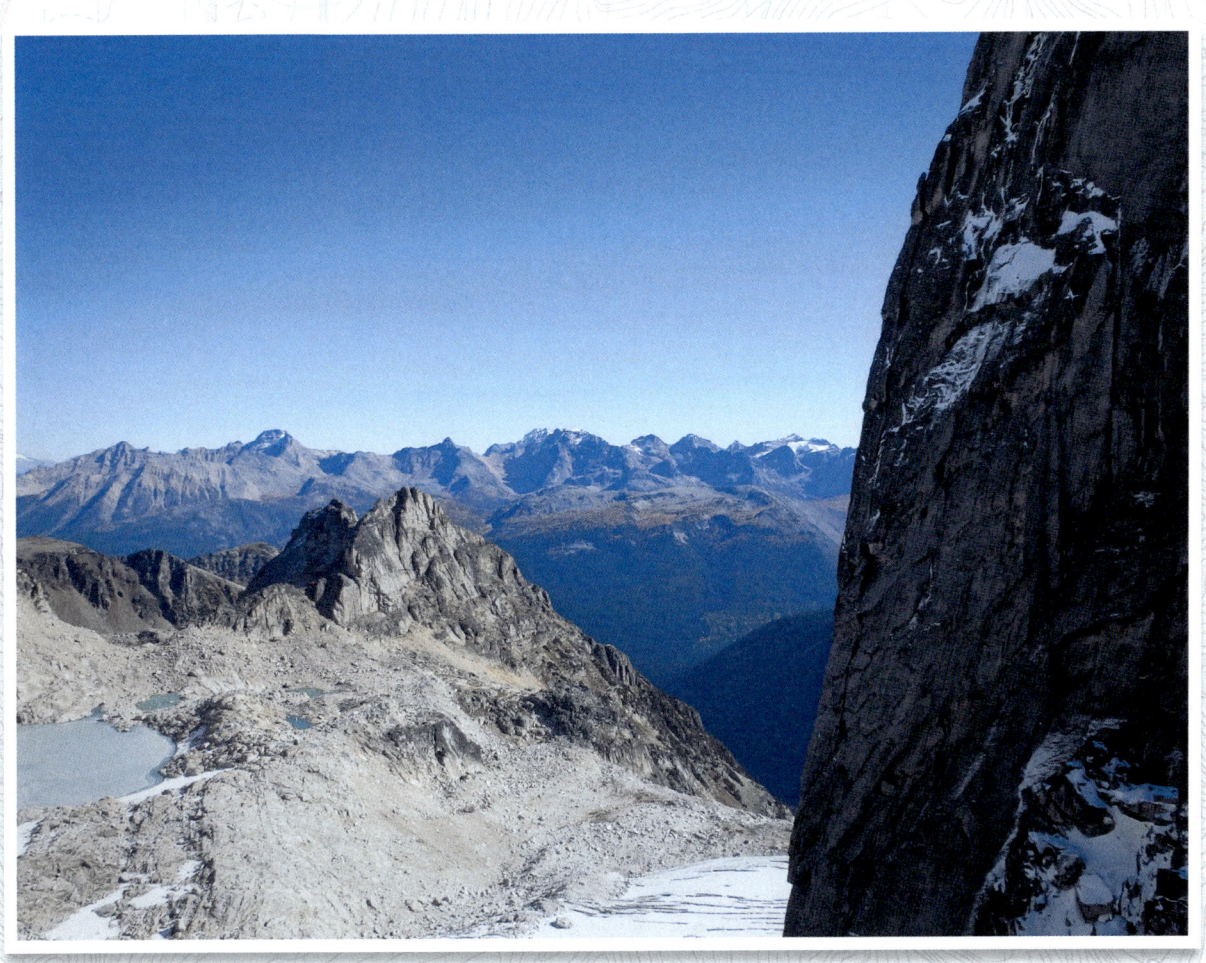

Poo With a View
Gavin T Boutet

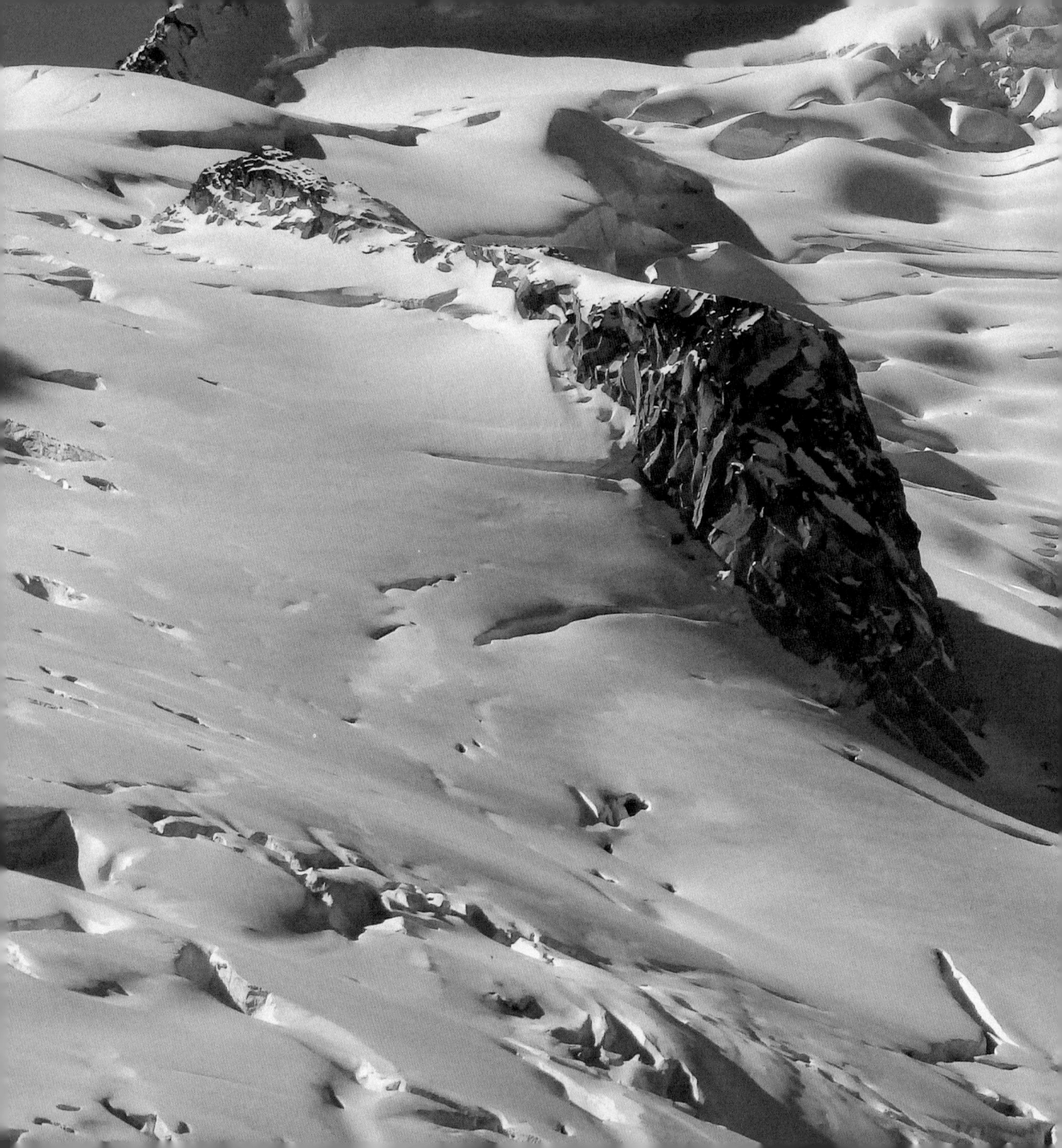

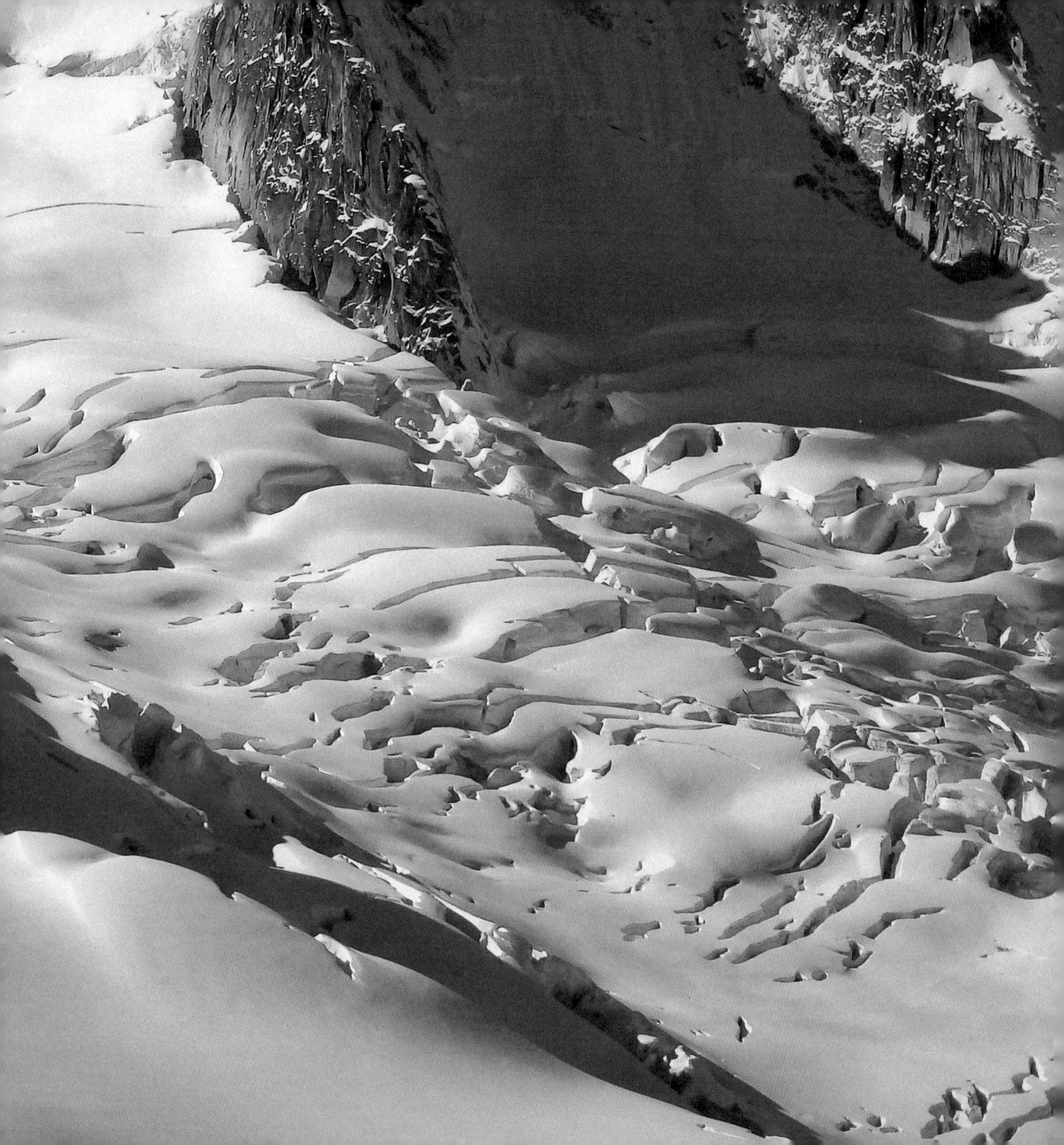

THE HIGHEST OUTHOUSE IN CANADA

2,955 m (9,695 ft)
Alberta/British Columbia border in Banff/Kootenay National Parks

Here's a fresh look at the new lavatory attached to the side of the Colgan Hut, the highest permanent structure in Canada. The large crevasses of Fay Glacier are only metres away from truly the most epic dump in the country. Take your time and enjoy the view!

Poo With a View
Gavin T Boutet

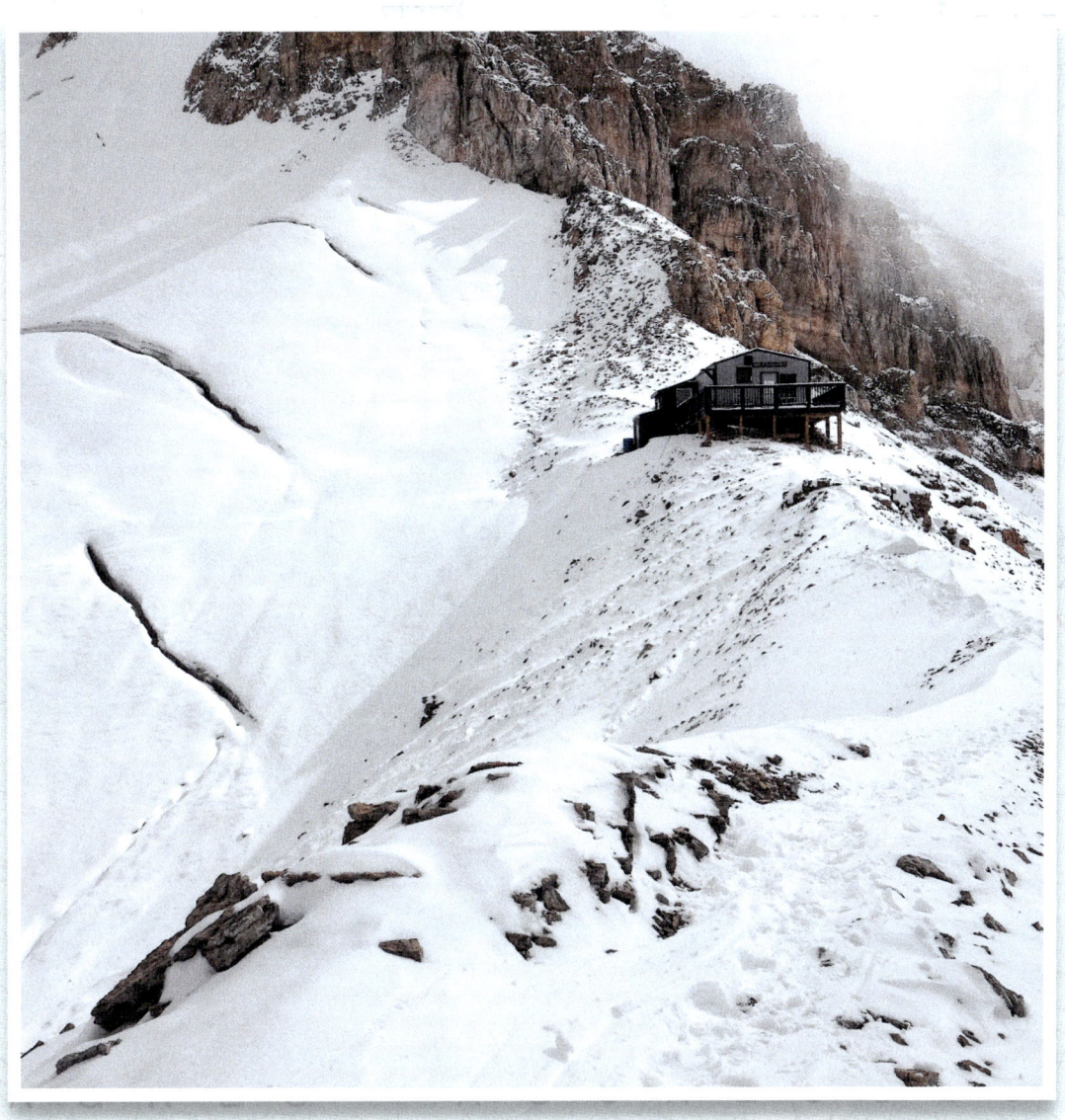

Poo With a View
Gavin T Boutet

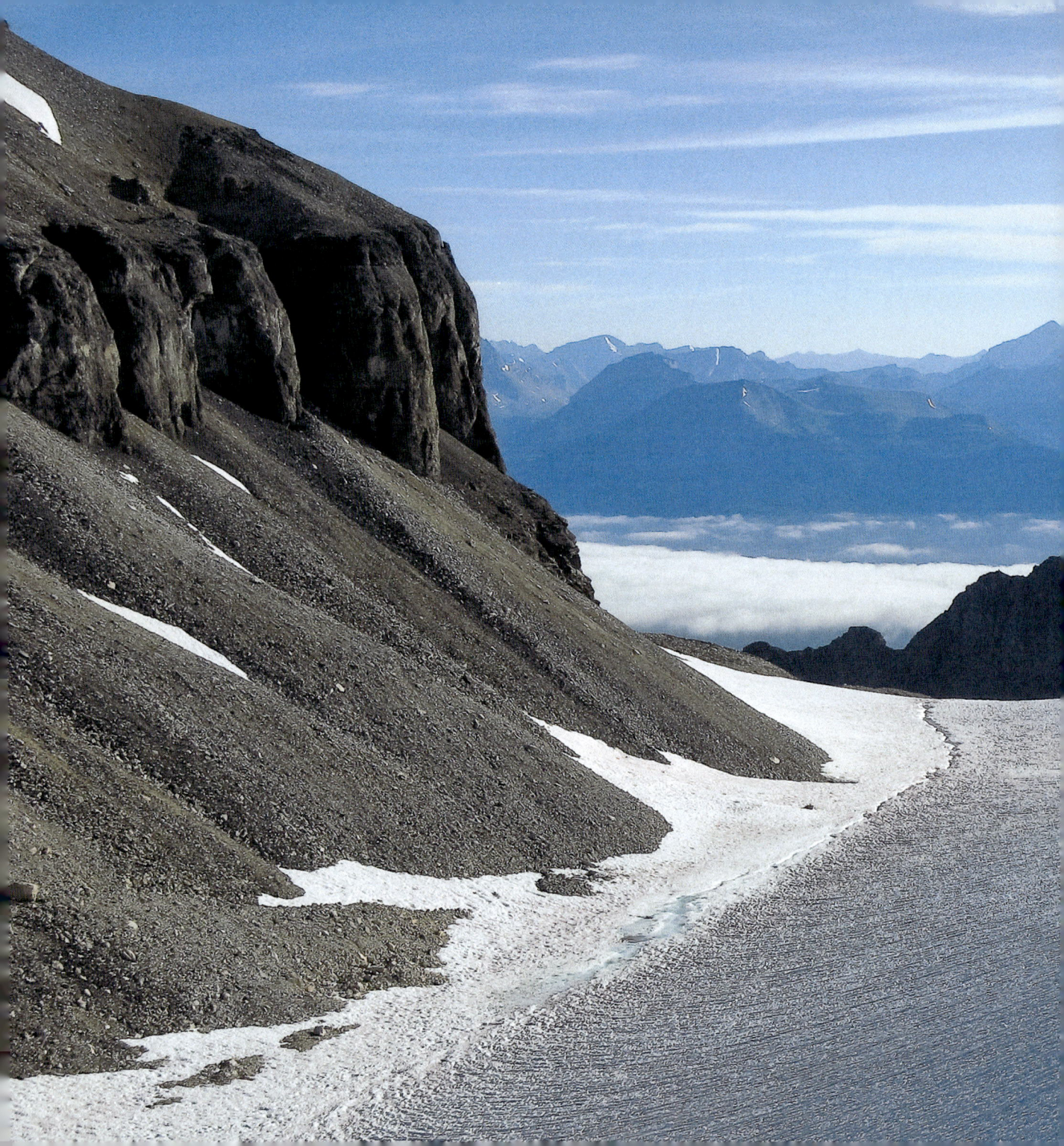

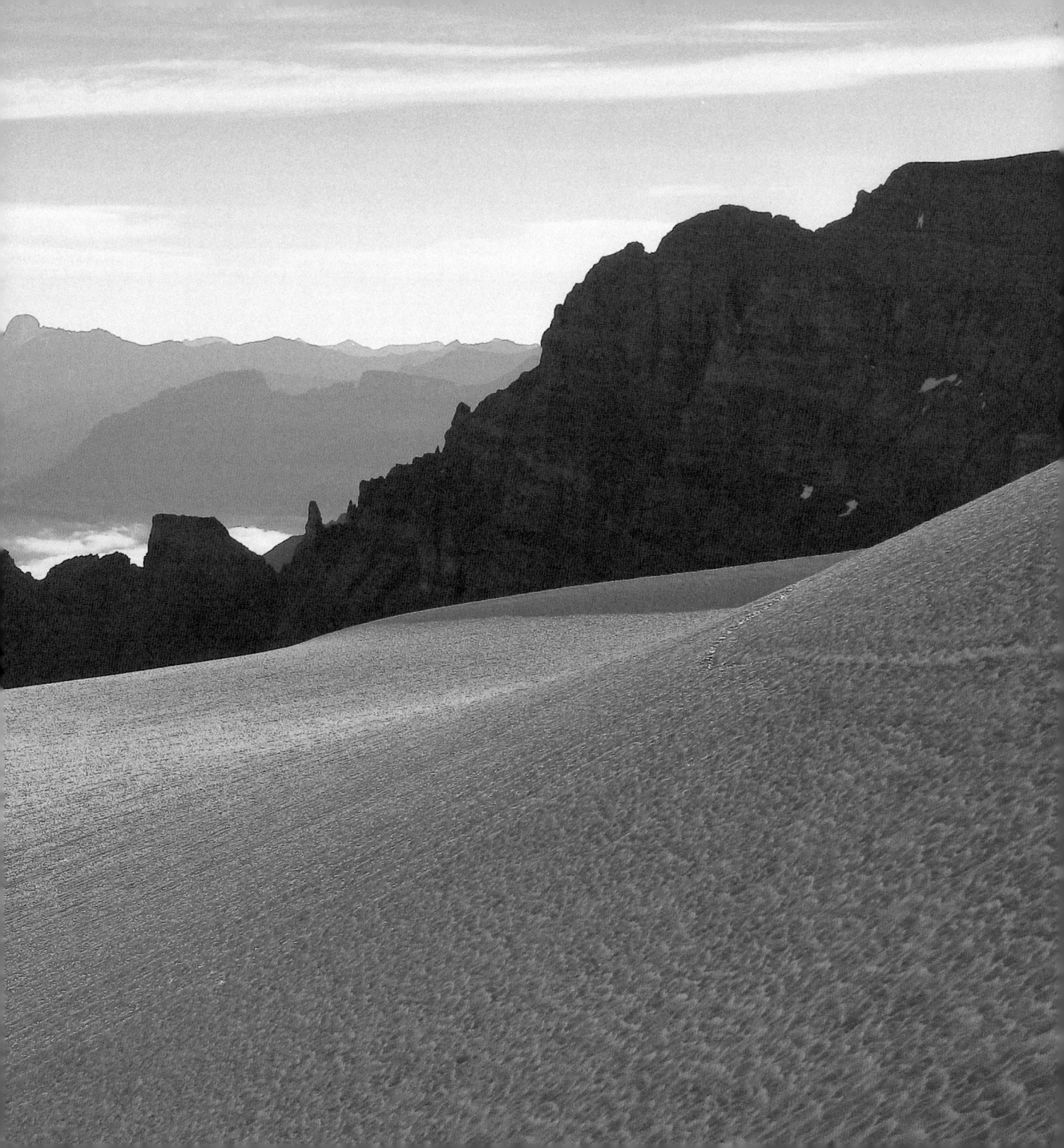

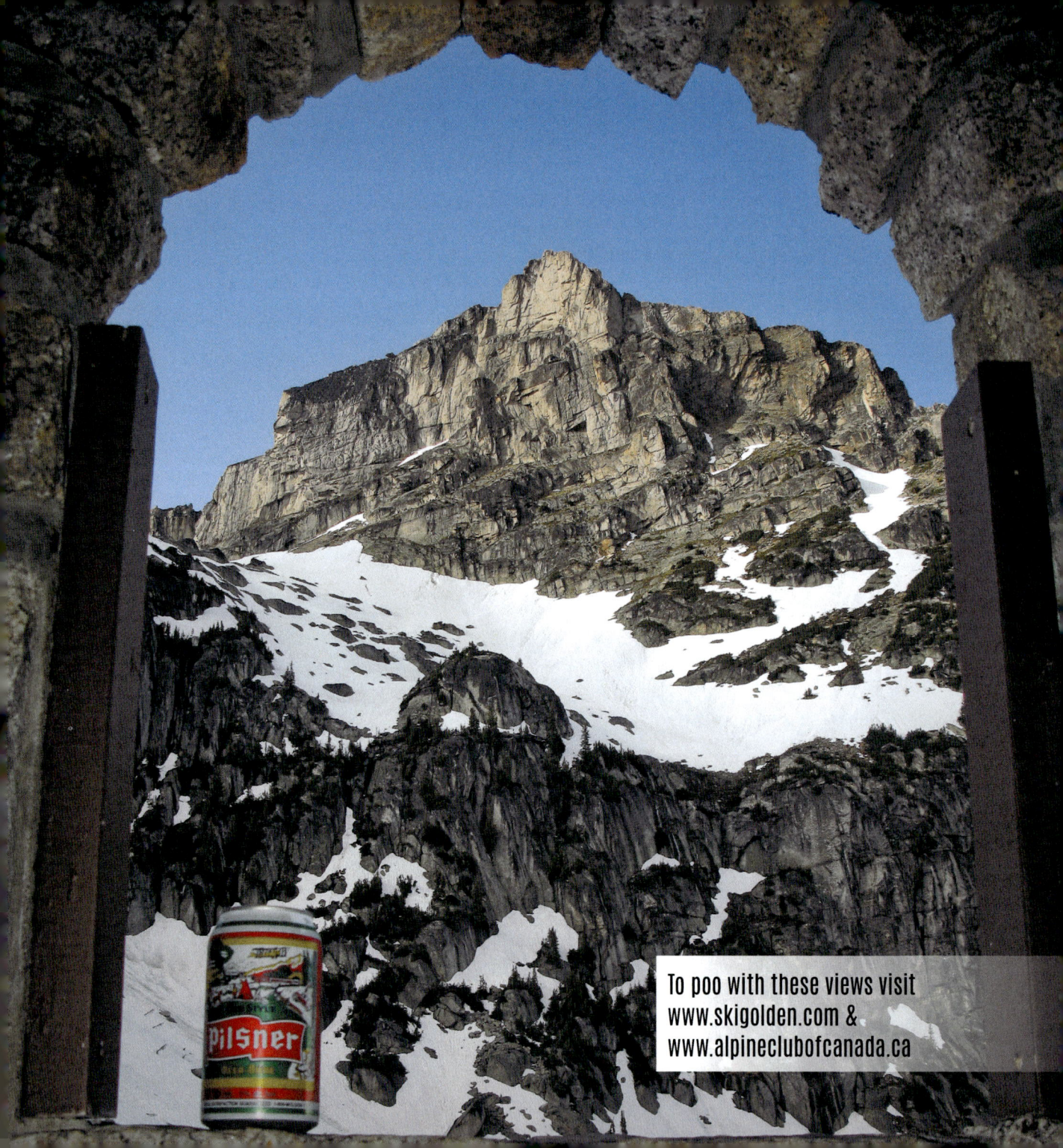

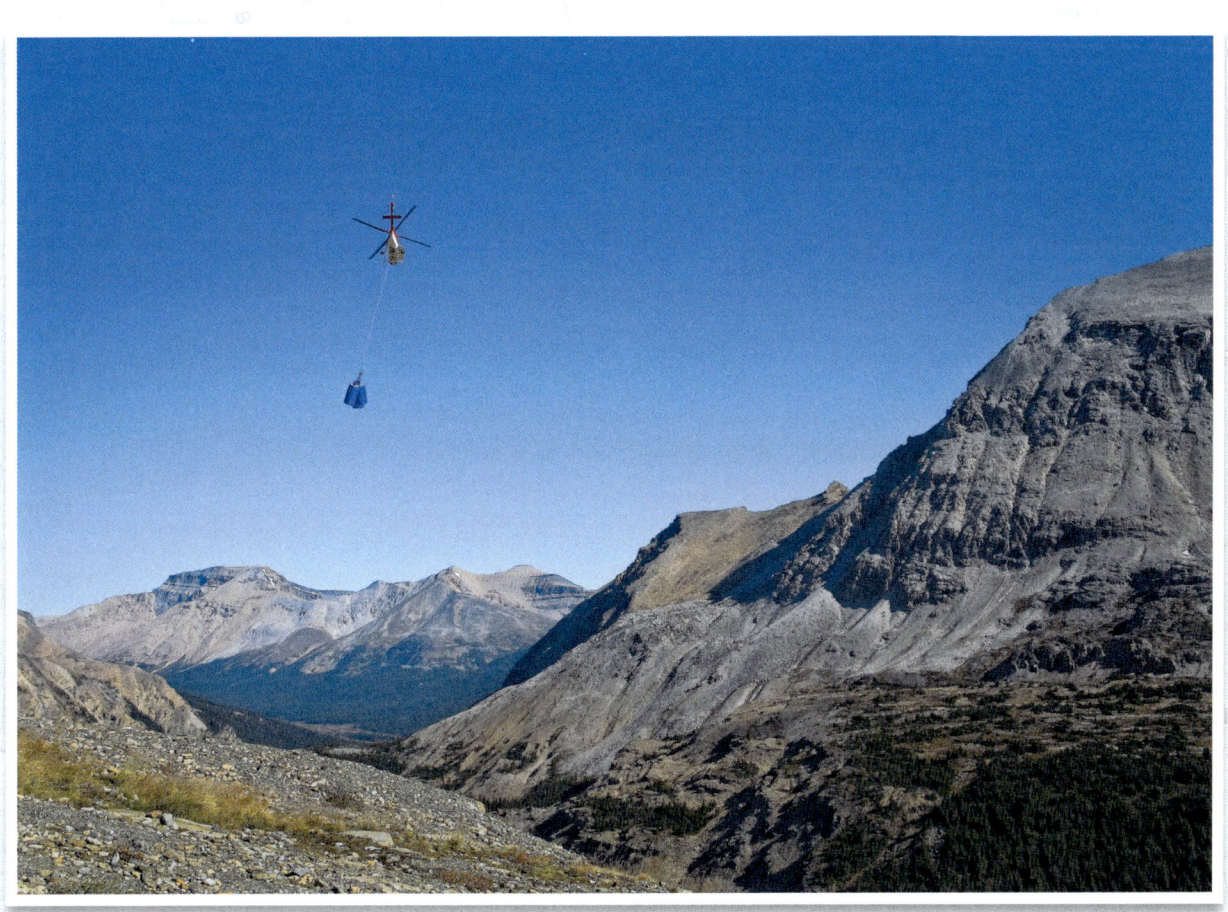

Poo With a View
Gavin T Boutet

Gavin T Boutet is a Collingwood, Ontario, native whose love for skiing brought him west into the spectacular Rocky Mountains of Alberta in 1999. Now residing in Canmore, just beyond the gates of Banff National Park, he works and plays in the mountains, fuelled by a fascination with nature and the outdoor environment. Gavin tends to focus his camera away from the mainstream to enlighten his audience with unusual perspectives from roads less travelled.

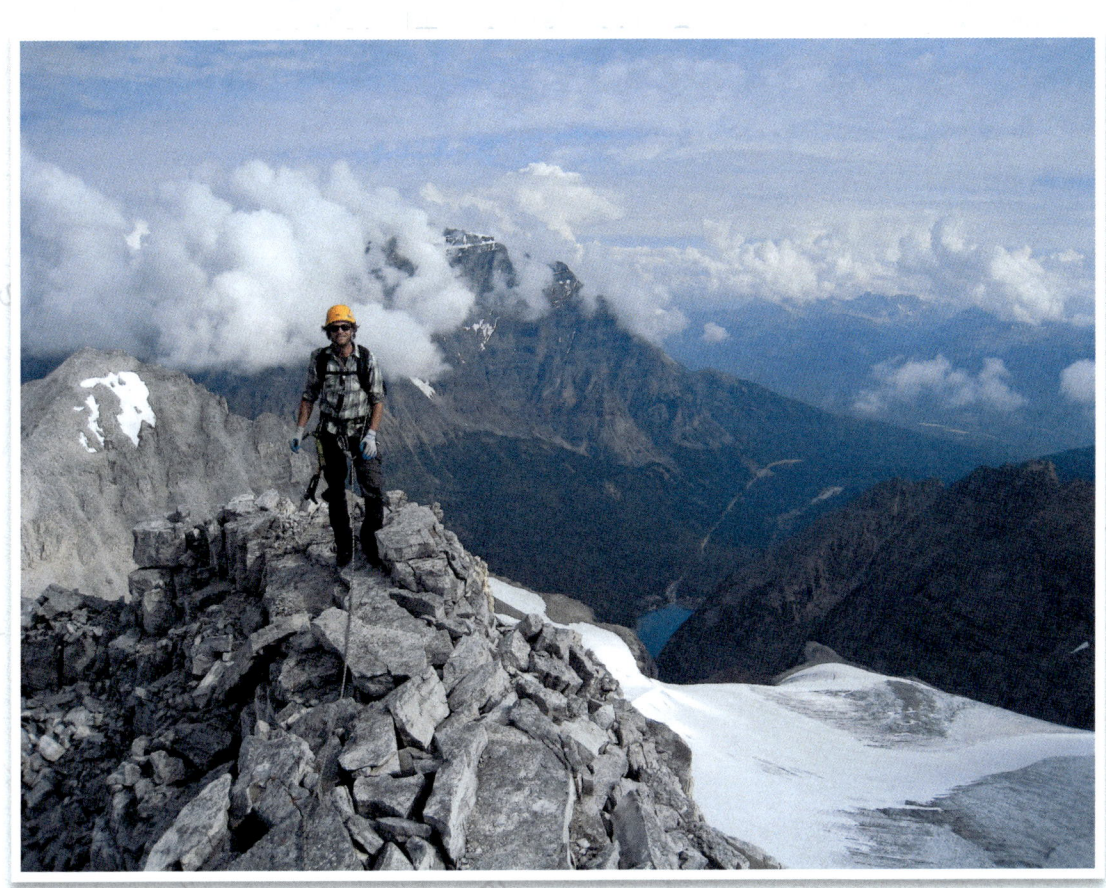

Author photo by Darren Enderwick

Manufactured by Amazon.ca
Bolton, ON